Mechanised Warfare in Colour

MILITARY TRANSPORT
of World War I
including Vintage Vehicles
and Post War Models

by
CHRIS ELLIS

illustrated by
DENIS BISHOP

BLANDFORD PRESS
POOLE   DORSET

First Published in 1970
Reprinted 1976

Copyright © 1970 Blandford Press Ltd.
Link House, West Street, Poole, Dorset BH15 1LL

ISBN 0 7137 0701 1

Colour section printed by Colour Reproduction Ltd., Billericay
Text filmset by Keyspools Ltd, Golborne, Warrington, Lancs.
Printed and bound in Great Britain by
Cox & Wyman Ltd, London, Fakenham and Reading

12
Sautter Harlé Pigeon Van, 1900–01, France

13
Davidson's Duryea Machine-Gun Car, 1899, U.S.A.

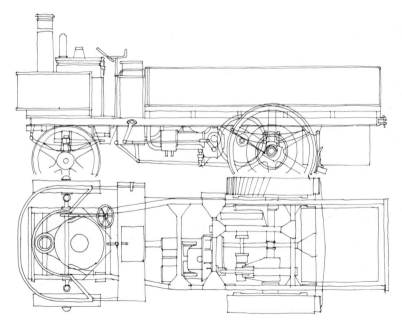

11
Thornycroft Steam Wagon (Types A and B), 1901, U.K.

9
Keller Tractor, 1900, Germany

10
Renault Car, 1900–01, France

7
Tracteur Scotte, 1894–98, France

8
McLaren 70-h.p. Traction Engine, 1899, U.K.

5
Fowler Road Locomotive, 1870, U.K./Germany

6
Fowler Artillery Siege Train Traction Engine, 1880, U.K.

4
Aveling and Porter Steam Sapper, 1871,
U.K./Russia/France/Turkey

Government Steam Train, 1870, U.K.

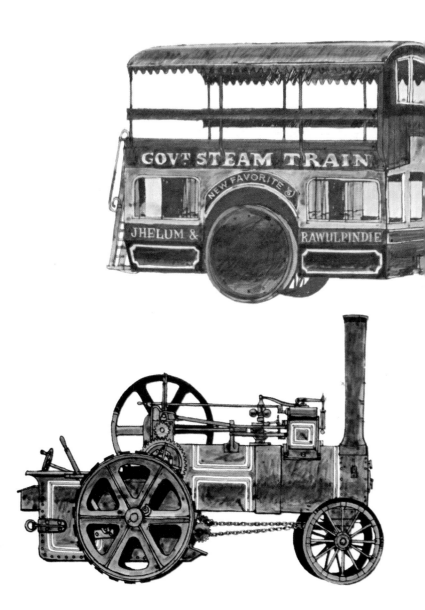

1
Burrell-Boydell Traction Engine, 1857, U.K.

2
Bray Patent Traction Engine, 1858, U.K.

were taking mechanised road transport into account in their forward planning. In both America and Britain exercise in 1908 involved the carriage of infantry in buses or lorries. Subsidy or subvention schemes were introduced in those years to make road vehicles widely available to the military forces in the event of war. How the subsidy schemes worked is briefly outlined in the main text, but suffice it to say here that these subsidy schemes benefited commerce as well as the army. For they set a standard for manufacturers to work to and the quality of lorry being used by 1914 was directly due to the military standards imposed by the subvention schemes. These schemes benefited commerce too, for they encouraged traders to buy transport vehicles which they might not otherwise be able to afford, they kept manufacturers in business—or at least encouraged them to expand their trade —and they overcame the usual peacetime limitations on military budgets, shortage of money. So the subsidy schemes enabled military authorities to collect together big fleets of vehicles at times of expansion and avoid having large sums of money tied up in fleets of trucks little used during peacetime.

The First World War saw the introduction of special purpose vehicles in large numbers—ambulances, repair trucks, staff cars, to mention just a few— a selection of contrasting types being illustrated here. This war saw the final emergence of the mechanised age, and road vehicles were built on an unprecedented scale. The coming of peace released floods of ex-military vehicles on

to the market and the mass production adopted during the war years became a normal technique for road vehicle manufacture. The subsidy schemes of the inter-war years assisted the manufacturers once more by laying down accepted standards for suspension, transmission, and bodywork. Also in a period of commercial slump the subsidy schemes kept manufacture ticking over.

This book ends at 1939 just before the major nations went to war again, and the vehicles which equipped the major nations before the new onslaught bring the book to a close. The next volume will deal exclusively with vehicles of the Second World War, but some of the vehicles shown here were used in that conflict or developed still further.

Deep technicalities are avoided as far as possible in this book, and strings of facts and figures are omitted since this is essentially a popular history telling the whys and wherefores of each vehicle's service and introduction rather than discussing the fine engineering standards involved. I have merely left in bare technical details sufficient for one vehicle to be compared with another. One other point in this context is that with many of the more obscure early vehicles included, technical facts and figures are scanty, if indeed any survive. The text can be read almost completely from beginning to end taking in all relevant developments over the period covered —which is why this introduction is brief —but the cross-headings and the listing at the back make it easy to locate any particular vehicle or its nationality without having to read all through the text.

INTRODUCTION

In the history of mechanised warfare—which really only begins with the present century—it is the tank and the armoured car which have captured popular imagination. Paradoxically the trucks, tractors, cars, and gun carriers which have really made warfare *mechanised* are in danger of being forgotten at the expense of the 'teeth' arms and the famous regiments which operate them. The trucks and other supporting vehicles are taken for granted, in fact, and probably only the Jeep of the Second World War fame is universally known as a military vehicle outside the tank and armoured car categories. The average layman has a vague recollection of trucks and staff cars seen in convoy or rushing round the countryside but even in a military parade all eyes are on the tanks and armoured cars.

However, the mundane transport and ancillary vehicles which support an army in battle have a history stretching back further than the tank by at least twice the span of time since the first tanks and armoured cars appeared. Indeed the very first practical mechanical road vehicle, Cugnot's steam carriage of 1782, was produced in the first place to tow guns, not just as a means of getting from A to B. Almost as soon as the steam traction engine had become a practical realisation it was being thought of by individuals as a replacement—partial at least—for the horse in heavy haulage work. The first few vehicles shown in this book cover this early period and the text points out the thinking which led to the adoption of steam traction by various military authorities and individuals. By 1870 traction engines had been used to tow guns, supplies, and even personnel under active service conditions and steam traction was to remain important to military forces until the Great War and beyond—in fact until the internal combustion engine had been developed sufficiently to power heavy haulage vehicles.

The perfection of the internal combustion engine in the 1890s led to the gradual adoption of cars by military authorities and in the early 1900s some imaginative soldiers like Genty in France and Davidson in America showed how cars could be used in an offensive role. Their cars equipped with guns predated the appearance of armoured cars by several years but they anticipated a role for the unarmoured patrol vehicle which was not widely accepted and did not become commonplace until the two World Wars took mechanised warfare into the desert and mountains. When the petrol engine became powerful enough the weight of armour could be carried on a normal chassis and the armoured car, fitted with guns, became a class of vehicle on its own, beyond the scope of this book. The Ehrhardt balloon destroyer of 1906 represents a key transitional vehicle for it appeared with both a normal tourer style of body (as we illustrate it) or with an armoured body. It was not the first armoured car, but it was one of the first.

Commercial petrol lorries appeared in numbers in the early 1900s and the military authorities in Germany, Britain France, and America were quick to see their value as store and troop carriers. By 1908–9 the use of petrol lorries was becoming commonplace and staff officers

PREFACE

This book is intended to complement those titles in the Blandford *Mechanised Warfare in Colour* series which are devoted to tanks and armoured vehicles by presenting a cavalcade of the less glamorous but equally essential non-combatant vehicles—trucks, tractors, and cars—which were used by the world's great fighting powers from the beginning of the mechanised era until 1939, which is as far as this present volume takes the story. The book is *not* a catalogue of all military vehicles, since at any one time there are thousands of different types in service throughout the world; merely listing all the military vehicles produced in the 1850–1939 period would more than fill this book even if any one individual could do so. Of necessity, therefore, I have had to be selective and I have chosen a good cross-section of types which qualify for inclusion on the strength of their technical, tactical, or functional significance, rather than on fame or looks alone.

The vehicles are arranged as nearly as possible in chronological order but some overlap is unavoidable, partly to assist in convenient arrangement of the contents and partly because so much concurrent development was happening over the period covered. One or two vehicles are deliberately shown out of strict sequence, mainly because the text deals with a group of closely related types and it is more logical to show a bunch of comparable types together.

However, just looking through the illustrations will give the reader a good visual idea of how military vehicles changed in shape, style, and function over a period of 70 years or so. Denis Bishop has arranged the individual drawings to make best use of the available page space, and so they are *not* to common scale.

For assistance in the preparation of this book both Denis Bishop and myself would like to thank Peter Chamberlain who sought out elusive visual references for some of the drawings. Similarly I would like to thank my brother Peter who tracked down other references on my behalf for some of the more obscure vehicles. Finally I would like to thank my wife for assistance in typing the manuscript.

In this new printing the opportunity has been taken to correct some small errors of fact which inevitably crept into the first printing. Several readers who had actual experience of some of these vehicles were kind enough to make comments and some of these have now been incorporated into the text. In this connection we must thank in particular Mr D. S. D. Williams, a Past President of the Diesel Engineers and Users Association, and M. Alain Gougaud.

CHRIS ELLIS

CONTENTS

14
Davidson's Steam Machine-Gun Car, 1902, U.S.A.

15
Cadillac Balloon Destroyer, 1908–10, U.S.A.

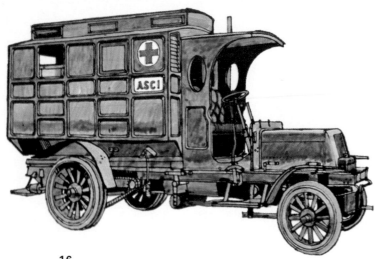

16
Straker-Squire Motor Ambulance Van, 1906–08, U.K.

17
Milnes-Daimler Motor Wagon, 1906–08, U.K.

18
Hannoversche Maschinenbau Steam Lorry, 1908, Germany

19
Train Renard, 1904, France

20
Above and opposite: Genty's Panhard Automitrailleuse, 1908,
France

21
Above and opposite: Armstrong-Whitworth Military Transport
Wagon, 1908, U.K.

22
Adler 25-cwt Light Lorry, 1908, Germany

23
Northover/Harley-Davidson Machine-Gun Carrier, 1908, Canada

24
Thornycroft 50-h.p. Heavy-oil Engine Tractor, 1909, U.K.

25
Broom & Wade 25-h.p. Military Tractor, 1909, U.K.

26
Milnes-Daimler Omnibus (Vanguard), 1908–09, U.K.

27
Napier Light Lorry, 1908–09, U.K.

28
Erhardt Balloon Destroyer, 1906, Germany

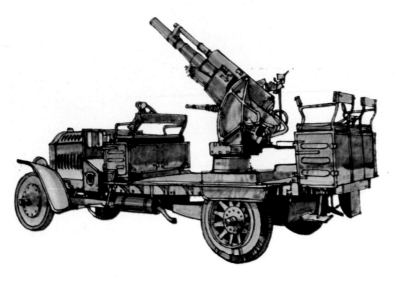

29
Krupp-Daimler Balloon Destroyer (7.5 cm. gun), 1909,
Germany

30
Packard 24-h.p. 3-ton Truck with Driggs-Schroeder Gun,
1909, U.S.A.

31
Packard 24-h.p. 3-ton Truck, 1909–18, U.S.A.

32
Ravaillier Amphibious Car, 1910, France

33
NAG 4-ton Lorry, Military Subvention Type, 1909–12, Germany

34
NAG 4-ton Lorry with Gas Containers, 1909–12, Germany

35
Napier Light Car, 1912, U.K.

36
Napier Light Car, 1912, U.K.

37
Hupmobile 20-h.p. Military Scout Car, 1912, U.S.A.

38
Foden 5-ton Steam Wagon, 1912, U.K.

39
Chatillon-Panhard Tractor, 1912–13, France

40
Lefebvre Tractor, 1913, France

41
Daimler Motor Bus, Tramway (M.E.T.) Omnibus Co., 1914,
U.K.

42
L.G.O.C. B Type Motor Bus/Lorry, 1914–18, U.K.

43
L.G.O.C. B Type Motor Bus, 1914–18, U.K.

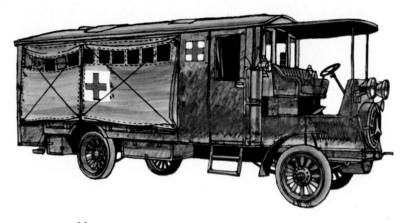

44
Boulant Mobile Surgery, 1912–18, France

45
Leyland 3-ton Subsidy A Van, 1914–18, U.K.

46
Foster-Daimler 105-h.p. Petrol Tractor, 1914–18, U.K.

47
Holt 75-h.p. Petrol Tractor, 1914–18, U.S.A./U.K./France

48
Renault Ambulance, 1914–18, France

49
Renault Searchlight Carrier, 1914–18, France

50
Jeffery Tractor, 1915–18, U.S.A./France/U.K.

51
Schneider PB2 Omnibus, 1914—18, France

52
Wolseley 3-ton Lorry, 1913—18, U.K.

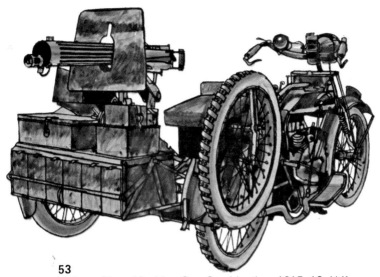

53
Vickers-Clyno Machine Gun Combination, 1915–18, U.K.

54a
Dennis 3-ton Lorry, 1913–18, U.K.

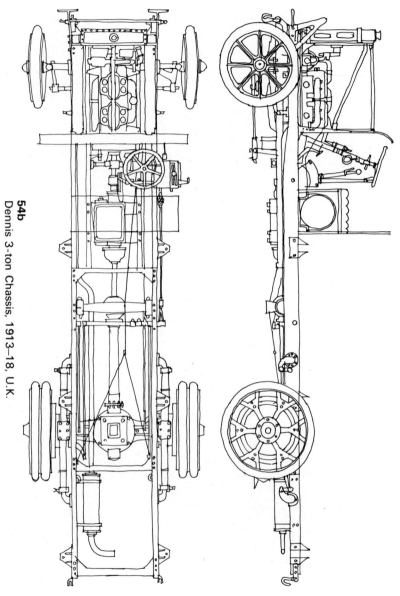

54b
Dennis 3-ton Chassis, 1913–18, U.K.

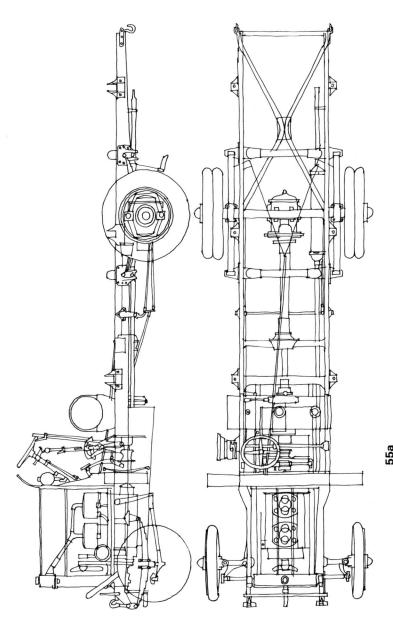

55a
Thornycroft 3-ton Lorry, J Type Chassis, 1913–18, U.K.

55b
Thornycroft 3-ton J Type Lorry with AA Gun, 1913–18, U.K.

56
Vauxhall D Type Staff Car, 1915–18, U.K.

57
Leyland Subsidy A Type, 1915–18, U.K.

58
Leyland Mobile Workshop, 1915–18, U.K.

59
Renault Porteur Tractor, 1916–18, France

60
Stoewer Staff Car, 1916–18, Germany

61
Latil Tractor, 1916–18, France/U.S.A.

62
Fiat 18BL Lorry, 1916–18, Italy

63
Fiat 18BL Generator Lorry, 1916–18, Italy

64
Mobile Searchlight, 1916–18, Italy

65
Latil Artillery Tractor, 1916–18, France/U.S.A.

66
Latil Artillery Tractor with Delahaye Tracks, 1918, France

67
Dodge Ambulance, 1917–19, U.S.A./U.K.

68
Dodge $\frac{1}{2}$-ton Light Repair Truck, 1917–19, U.S.A./U.K.

69
Ford Model T Light Patrol Car, 1915–19, U.S.A./U.K.

70
Ford Model T Rail Tractor, 1916–18, U.K.

71
White Reconnaissance Car, 1917–19, U.S.A.

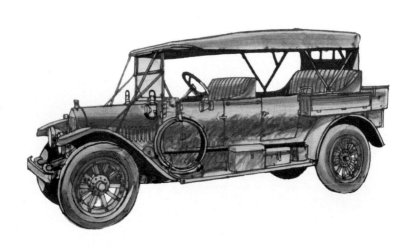

72
White Observation Car, 1917–19, U.S.A.

73
$2\frac{1}{2}$-ton Tractor, 1918–19, U.S.A.

74
5-ton Tractor, 1918–19, U.S.A.

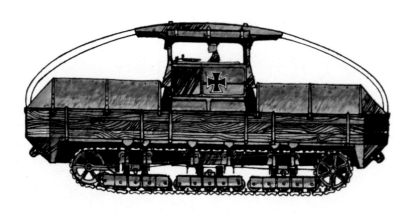

75
A7V Überlandwagen, 1917–18, Germany

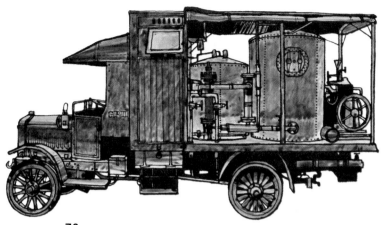

76
Riker 3-ton Lorry, 1917–18, U.S.A./U.K.

77
Commer Ambulance, 1916–18, U.K.

78
Crossley Staff Car, 1918, U.K.

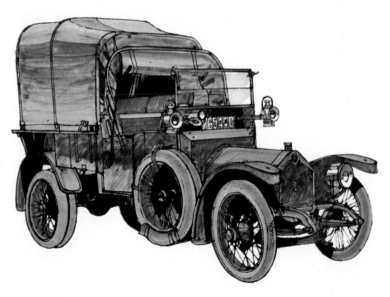

79
Crossley Tender, 1918, U.K.

80
F.W.D. Model B 3-ton Lorry, 1916–18, U.S.A./U.K.

81
F.W.D. Artillery Supply Truck, 1917–18, U.S.A.

82
F.W.D. Artillery Repair Truck, 1917–18, U.S.A.

83
F.W.D. Ordnance Repair Truck, 1917–18, U.S.A.

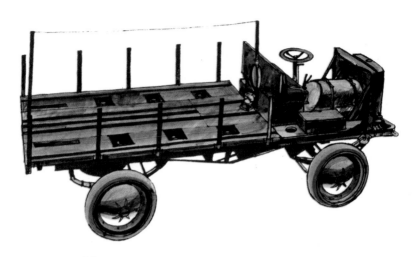

84
Jeffery 240-mm. Mortar Carrier, 1918, U.S.A.

85
Liberty Four-Wheel Drive Truck, 1916–18, U.S.A./U.K.

86
Liberty Class B 5-ton Truck (converted to six wheels), 1919,
U.S.A.

87
Liberty Class C 5-ton Truck, 1920, U.S.A.

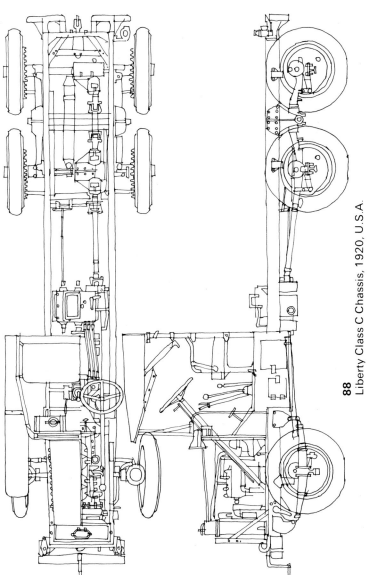

88

Liberty Class C Chassis, 1920, U.S.A.

89
F.W.D. Model B Ordnance Maintenance Truck, 1920, U.S.A.

90
Citroen-Kegresse prototype, 1923, France

91a
Citroen-Kegresse Line-Layer, 1925, U.K.

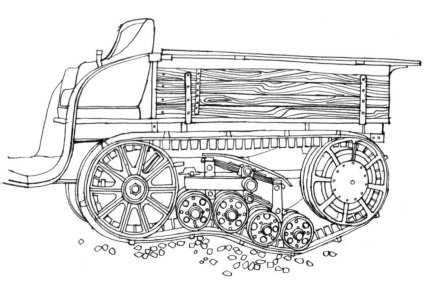

91b
Kegresse suspension unit, 1925, U.K.

92
Burford-Kegresse Artillery Tractor, 1926, U.K.

93
Burford-Kegresse Truck, 1926, U.K.

94
Morris-Roadless 1-ton Truck, 1926, U.K.

95
Guy-Roadless 1-ton Truck, 1926, U.K.

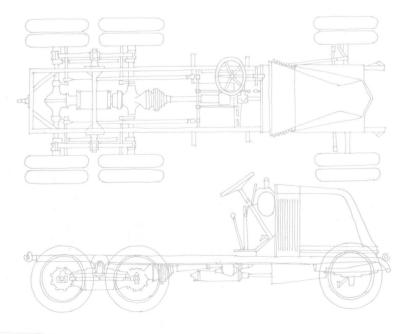

96
Renault 12-cwt Dragon, 1926, France/U.K.

97
T.T.S.W. 1½-ton Truck, 1926, U.S.A.

98
Dragon Mark I Gun Tractor, 1924, U.K.

99
Dragon Mark II Gun Tractor, 1926, U.K.

100a
Vickers-Wolseley Staff Car, 1926, U.K.

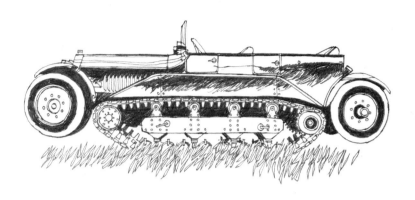

100b
Vickers-Wolseley Staff Car running on its tracks, 1926, U.K.

101
Light D Tank, 1923, U.K.

102a
Pavesi P4, 1913, Italy/France

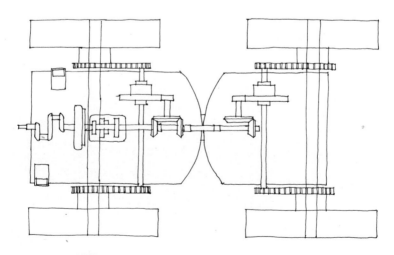

102b
Pavesi P4 Chassis

103
Pavesi Gun Tractor, 1926, Italy

104
Pavesi Tractor Mark 1, 1926, U.K.

105
Karrier WO6 Medium Lorry, 1926, U.K.

106
Crossley 3-ton Medium Lorry, 1926, U.K.

107a
Morris-Commercial D Type Light Lorry, 1928, U.K.

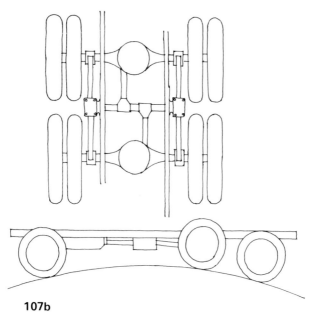

107b
W.D. Patent Articulating Rear Bogie, 1928, U.K.

108
Morris-Commercial D Type Wireless Van, 1928, U.K.

109
Morris-Commercial CD Type, 1932, U.K.

110
Citroen P.17 Machine-Gun Carrier, 1931, France/U.S.A.

111
Citroen P.17 Gun Tractor, 1931, France/U.S.A.

112
Citroen P.14 Breakdown
Truck, 1928–32, France

113
Ceirano Auto-Cannone 75 mm., 1929, Italy

114
Trojan Light Six-Wheeler, 1929, U.K.

115
Hathi Tractor, 1927–33, U.K.

116
Hathi Tractor, 1927–33, U.K.

117
F.W.D. Gun Tractor, 1932, U.K.

118
F.W.D. Tractor, 1932, U.K.

119a
Latil TL Tractor, 1935, France

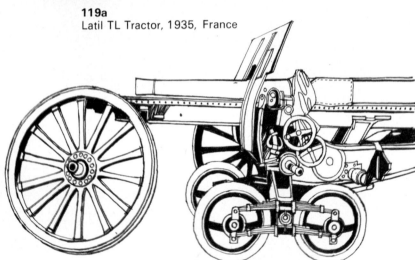

119b
Train Rouleur Bogie for towed gun carriages, 1935, France

120
Latil KTL Tractor, 1936, France

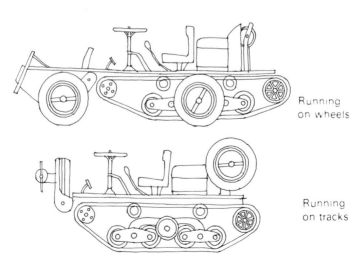

Running
on wheels

Running
on tracks

121
A.D.M.K. Mulus, 1935, Austria

122
Henschel Medium Truck, 1930, Germany

123
Steyr 40D Light Truck, 1934, Austria

124
Horch Radio Car, Kfz 17, 1934, Germany

125
Mercedes Light Repair Car, Kfz 2/40, 1936, Germany

126
Leichter Zugkraftwagen 3-ton HL KL 2, 1932, Germany

127
Sd Kfz 11 Half-Track, 1936, Germany

128
Sd Kfz 11/1 Nebelkraftwagen, 1939, Germany

129
Kfz 12 Utility Car, 1934, Germany

130
Mittlerer Zugkraftwagen, Sd Kfz 6, 1936, Germany

131
Mittlerer Zugkraftwagen, Sd Kfz 6, 1936, Germany

132
Mittlerer Zugkraftwagen Sd Kfz 7, 1937, Germany

133
Mittlerer Zugkraftwagen Sd Kfz 7/6, 1937, Germany

134
3-ton General Service Truck, A.E.C. Marshal, 1936–40, U.K.

135
3-ton Bridging Truck, A.E.C. Marshal, 1936–40, U.K.

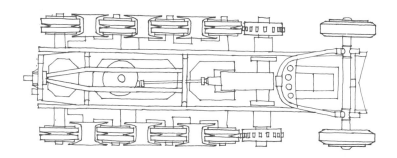

136
Schwerer Zugkraftwagen, 12-ton, Sd Kfz 8, 1936–45,
Germany

137
Somua MCL5 Tractor, 1936, France

138
Somua MCL5 Artillery Tractor, 1936, France

139
Laffly G35T Artillery Tracteur 1934, France

140
Lorraine 28, 1936, France

141
Tracteur Latil TAR 5, 1932–36, France

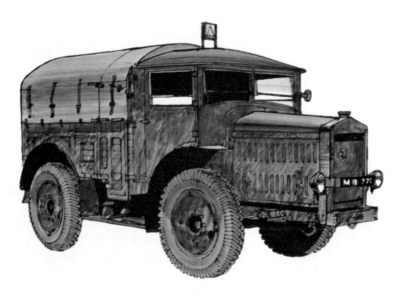

142
Tracteur Latil TAR H, 1932–36, France

143
Amphibious Car, Texier de la Caillerie, 1934, France

144
Scammell 6 × 4 Artillery Tractor, 1932–40, U.K.

145
Morris-Commercial 6 × 4 Artillery Tractor, 1936, U.K.

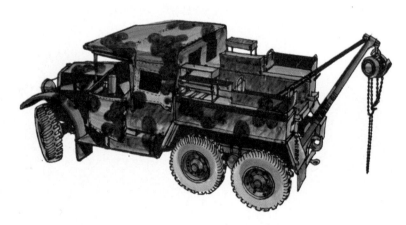

146
Morris-Commercial 6 × 4 30-cwt Light Breakdown, 1938
U.K.

147
Bedford 15-cwt Truck, 1938, U.K.

148
Bedford 15-cwt Water Tanker, 1939, U.K.

149
BMW R75 Motor Cycle, 1937—40, Germany

150
Zundapp KS750 Motor Cycle, 1937—40, Germany

151
Kfz 69, Horch, 1938, Germany

152
Kfz 11 Utility Car, 1938, Germany

153
Morris 8-cwt Wireless Truck, 1935–38, U.K.

154
Morris 15-cwt Platoon Truck, 1935–38, U.K.

155
Guy 'Ant' 15-cwt Truck, 1935, U.K.

156
Guy 'Quad-Ant' Field Artillery Tractor, 1938, U.K.

157
Mercedes-Benz G4 Staff Car, 1936, Germany

158
Norton Motor Cycle Combination, 1938–39, U.K.

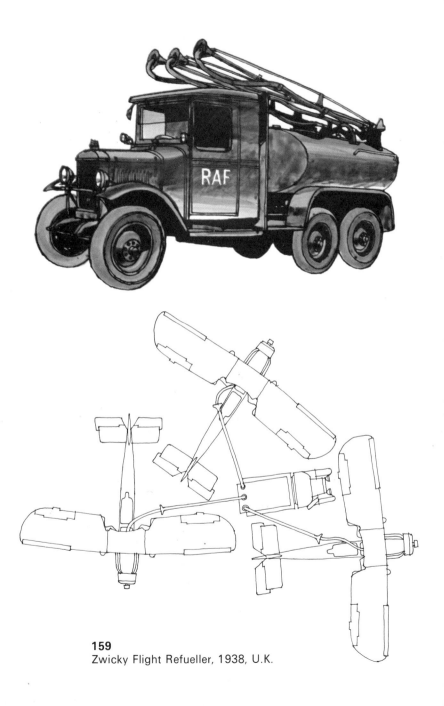

159
Zwicky Flight Refueller, 1938, U.K.

160
GAZ-AA, from 1932, Russia

161
GAZ-AAA, from 1932, Russia

162
ZIS-5, from 1933, Russia

163
Isuzu Type 94, from 1935, Japan

SERVICE DES POSTES
3 ARMÉE 9 DIVISION

SERVICE DES RECONNAISANCE
...MITRAILLEUSE LEGERES
DIVISION DE CAVALLERIE ...

164
French vehicle markings, pre-1914

165
British Army markings, 1916

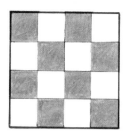

166
British Corps and Divisional emblems, 1916–18

167
British and American vehicle markings, 1917–18

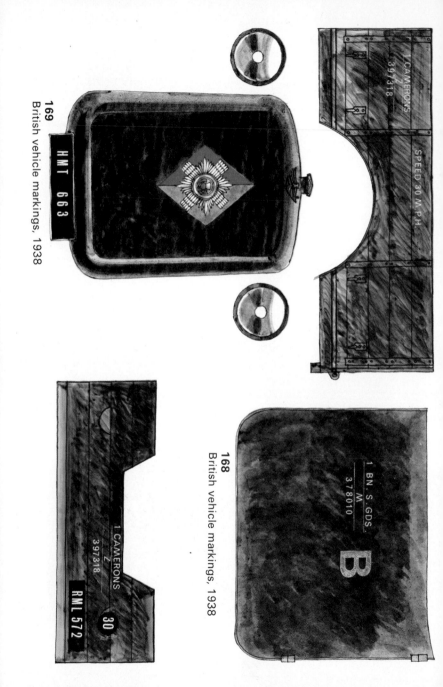

169
British vehicle markings, 1938

168
British vehicle markings, 1938

1 CAMERONS
397318

SPEED 30 M.P.H.

HMT 663

1·BN·S·GDS.
M
378010

B

1 CAMERONS
Z
397318

30

RML 572

DESCRIPTIVE NOTES

1 Burrell-Boydell Traction Engine, 1857, U.K.

One of the first practical traction engines to interest military authorities of any nation was the Burrell-Boydell machine, two of which were purchased for trials by the British Government in 1857. The distinctive characteristic of this design was the type of shoe, or 'endless railway' which had been evolved and patented by James Boydell some years previously. These 'endless railway' shoes, attached to the wheels, were intended in the first instance to assist traction when the engine was used for ploughing over rough fields. Though not conceived with any military purpose in view, Boydell's 'endless railway' is of interest since it anticipated by some years the 'crawler track' idea later used on cross-country tractors and subsequently adopted for the tanks evolved in the First World War. Boydell's 'endless railway' shoes were each made of wood and faced with iron. They were shaped roughly like a human foot (complete with 'big toe'), leading to the early description of 'footed wheels.' On the centre-line of the back of each shoe was a 'cycloidal' rail, corresponding in function to the human ankle, which was pivoted to a bracket on the wheel rim and took up or laid down each shoe as the wheel revolved. The size of the shoes was worked out mathematically to suit the diameter of the wheel to which they were fitted.

Charles Burrell, of Thetford in Norfolk, England, made his first traction engine with Boydell footed wheels in 1855. At this time Britain was involved in the Crimean War and sets of Boydell shoes were ordered and used in the Crimea attached to the wheels of heavy horse-drawn carts in the very muddy conditions encountered. This led to the suggestion that a Burrell traction engine so fitted should be taken to the Crimea to replace the horses. One far-seeing Englishman at this time, James Cowen, even went so far as to suggest that the engine should be fitted with an armour cover, have scythes fitted to its wheel hubs, and carry guns. This idea was rejected by the authorities at the time, however, as 'barbaric'. In the event, the war was over before anything further could be done. However, two Burrell-Boydell engines were purchased by the War Department and these were tested, and subsequently used, at the Woolwich Arsenal and adjacent dockyard for a short period in 1857–58. One test involved towing a siege gun and limber, complete with 16-man crew, from the Arsenal to Plumstead Common, with severe grades in each direction. A major failing was revealed in Boydell's 'endless rails' in that they broke easily on hard surfaces. Similarly large stones could cause the cycloidal rail to twist, since it had no lateral flexibility, and this again could immobilise the vehicle. As a result the Burrell-Boydell traction engines were quickly sold off by the War Department and it was some years before any military authority became interested once more in vehicles with such a potentially good cross-country performance.

The Burrell-Boydell vehicle shown

weighed about 9-tons and had a single speed. It was steered by a tiller on the front axle which was controlled by chains from the marine-type steering wheel.

2 Bray Patent Traction Engine, 1858, U.K.

William Bray was a contemporary of Burrell and, possibly inspired by the Boydell patent, evolved another and more ingenious means of providing extra grip for the wheels of a traction engine. Bray was chief engineer of a cross-channel paddle steamer and developed a wheel something like a paddle wheel, except that the blades could be moved in and out through the rim of the wheel as necessary to provide some extra grip on rough arable surfaces. Bray patented his device on 31 December 1856. It consisted of a normal iron-spoked wheel with the rim in the form of a trough with cut-out slots for the blades. A boss was fixed eccentrically to the wheel axle and rods were arranged round the boss connected flexibly to the blades within the trough-shaped rims. The position of the eccentric boss relative to the outer rim could be changed by means of worm gear from the driving position. The outer part of the wheel free-wheeled so that as the wheels rotated the blades moved out through their slots on one side of the rim and retracted on the opposite side. For cross-country running the eccentric was adjusted so that the blades protruded on the downward turn of the wheel and retracted on the upward turn. For running on roads the eccentric was turned round so that the blades protruded on the upward turn and retracted

on the downward turn. This in-and-out action of the blades also served to clear them of mud. The projection of the blades could be adjusted from $\frac{3}{4}$ inch to 3 inch. A prototype vehicle was built on Bray's behalf by local craftsmen in Folkestone, his home town. The Bray Traction Engine was completed in early 1858 and after some successful commercial trials, the War Department took an interest, the Burrell-Boydell machine having been rejected. In May 1858 the Bray engine was tested at Woolwich Arsenal when it was used to haul three 68-pdr. guns, a total weight of 20 tons. The steeply inclined route was the same as had been followed by the Burrell-Boydell engine. The illustration shows the Bray Traction Engine on this particular occasion and the blades protruding through the rims of the main wheels can clearly be seen. Though the Bray engine performed well at these trials and attained speeds of $2\frac{1}{2}$ m.p.h. for a modest consumption of coke, the War Department did not actually order any Bray engines for service. The Admiralty did, however, and purchased at least two for use at Woolwich and Keyham dockyards where they were mainly used for hauling heavy machinery and components like ships' propellers. The Bray engine weighed about 7 tons.

3 Government Steam Train, 1870, U.K.

A young engineer officer, Lieutenant R. E. Crompton, was responsible for much progress in the adoption of mechanised road haulage for military purposes. Crompton was an inventive young man who commanded the British Army's engineering workshop at Rawalpindi in India. He had built a primitive steam wagon in his spare time and this worked with a fair amount of success, leading him to the opinion that there was a definite military potential for steam tractors to haul guns, stores, and troops. Crompton followed engineering developments in Britain and was much impressed with accounts of a small rubber-tyred steam tractor which had demonstrated great hauling powers on trial. This vehicle was the Thomson Road Steamer, designed by a Scottish engineer, R. W. Thomson. Thomson was one of the first to see the value of rubber tyres and he had patented a 'solid' tyre of soft india rubber which was held to the wheel by narrow steel strips. The tyres were actually made up of small rubber 'shoes' held together with links round the wheel rims. The Road Steamer was a very simple vehicle, featuring a small single front wheel for steering and twin wheels of large diameter at the rear. A vertical 'coffee pot' boiler powered two cylinders, and these drove the rear wheels. The rubber tyres did, in fact, give a poor grip when the vehicle was driven across country, but the vehicle excelled on well made roads.

In India the roads were relatively well made and Lieutenant Crompton's idea was that vehicles of the Thomson type should be purchased and used in place of the ox and mule teams which at that time, there being few railways in India, made movement of stores between the garrisons a long and protracted business. Crompton put his ideas to the military commanders who eventually agreed to put his idea to the test. A Thomson Road Steamer was borrowed and a department was formed to operate it under the title of Government Steam Train, with Crompton in charge. The Thomson Road Steamer arrived in late 1869 and was put to the test, towing the existing carts. In practice the steam vehicle was not a great success; in Britain it burned coal but in India only wood was available and the firebox was not big enough for the vast amount of wood required to raise the equivalent head of steam. Hence there were frequent stops to raise steam and the net improvement in travelling time, compared to ox-drawn carts, was minimal. The military authorities were prepared to terminate trials there and then, but Crompton managed to get the backing of the Governor-General of Simla to allow extended trials with bigger Road Steamers. It was agreed that Crompton should go to England to see Thomson and arrange for an improved design of vehicle to meet Indian conditions. Crompton arrived early in 1870 and found that a larger improved vehicle was already being built for the military authorities in England and was to be used at Woolwich Arsenal. This vehicle, *Advance,* retained the same layout as the earlier Road Steamers and had rear wheels 6 foot in diameter and a 4-foot front wheel. It also had the vertical 'coffee pot' boiler with twin cylinders driving a crankshaft which drove the rear wheels. The crankshaft gave only one high gearing, and for low gearing a parallel countershaft was engaged. Crompton ordered two similar vehicles for his Government Steam Train department, though he asked for a horizontal Field boiler which gave a bigger grate area for wood burning than the vertical boiler. However, Thomson insisted on a vertical boiler, at least for the two initial engines.

The Government Steam Train engines, *Chenab* and *Ravee* were built by Ransome's of Ipswich and the first, *Chenab,* was completed in May 1871. While this vehicle performed well enough on coal, during its trials, it was evident that the vertical boiler would not be able to raise sufficient steam with wood. Hence Crompton arranged with another firm to make new Field boilers which could be used as retrospective replacements. Ransomes now took *Chenab* on a tour of the various engineering shows and engine trials and a twin-wheel omnibus trailer was built in Edinburgh as a prototype for the 'train' which *Chenab* was to haul. Suitably marked 'Govt Steam Train', 'Jhelum & Rawalpindi', the bus trailer was a two-decker. It was intended that troops or government officials would ride on the top deck and carry their equipment (and also sleep) in the lower deck. *Chenab* was extensively tested in England, but though speeds of 5 m.p.h. were attained there were many problems with maintaining steam. The illustration shows *Chenab* at this time. Crompton eventually rejected *Chenab* and sent her back to the makers for modification, turning his attention to the second vehicle *Ravee,* for which a Field boiler was now ready. Thomson would not allow boilers other than the 'coffee pot' type unless Crompton could convince him that *Ravee* was at least as good a performer as *Chenab*. Crompton demonstrated that *Ravee* was indeed a practical proposition with the new boiler by making the acceptance trial into one of the longest runs until then undertaken with a traction engine, a journey from Ipswich to Edinburgh and back. This took place in September-October 1871, with the return trip in November. It was an impressive success with a total distance exceeding 850 miles and an average speed at one stage of over 9 m.p.h.; at one point 25 m.p.h. was attained. Trials in Edinburgh took up three weeks, after which construction of two more steamers was ordered and Crompton returned to India. The first vehicle arrived in India in the spring of 1872, and the Government Steam Trains operated for several years until there was a sufficiently large railway network to render them unnecessary. In India the steamers hauled trains of several trailers and omnibuses, but four-wheelers were mostly used rather than the two-wheeler illustrated. Subsequently, in 1871-72, Thomson Road Steamers were also supplied to the governments of Turkey, Greece, and Russia where they were used for 'steam trains' in a similar fashion. These later engines all had horizontal boilers. The awning, however, was peculiar to the Government Steam Train vehicles operating in the hot conditions of India.

4 Aveling and Porter Steam Sapper, 1871, U.K./Russia/France/Turkey.

This vehicle had the distinction of being the first traction engine designed specifically for military use. Previous to this military authorities had simply purchased or hired commercial types on those few occasions when heavy haulage had been required. In Britain in 1869, however, a committee was appointed by the War Office, under a Colonel Galwey, to consider the possibility of adopting traction engines for military service on a regular basis. In Easter that same year two borrowed traction engines had been used by volunteer battalions to haul guns in a mock attack on Dover Castle. The committee decided that traction engines, if adopted, would be the Royal Engineers' responsibility. The major use for which the employment of traction engines was envisaged was the haulage of heavy artillery. At that time the heaviest gun in British service was the 95-cwt Armstrong breech-loader. This weapon on its field carriage weighed 5 tons 12 cwt and Royal Engineers pontoon—bridging equipment was available to take this load. It was desirable that any military traction engine should not exceed this weight so that the same pontoon equipment could be used. The firm of Aveling and Porter, of Rochester, Kent, who were located near the Royal Engineers depot, undertook to produce a machine with good hauling power but within the specified weight limits. The first vehicle was demonstrated at the Royal Agricultural Show in June 1871 where it attracted considerable attention by virtue of its relatively diminutive size and sturdy hauling power. With a weight of only 4 tons 5 cwt empty (5 tons in working order) it was a nominal 6-h.p. machine with conventional locomotive type boiler. The rear wheels were 5 feet in diameter and the front wheels 3½ feet. A second vehicle was ordered for official military trials and this was delivered in September 1871, by which time the type was being popularly called the 'Steam Sapper'. This second machine was altered slightly in an attempt to reduce its weight even more. The major change was a smaller water tank, reduced from 120 gallons in

capacity to 70 gallons. This lowered the weight of the vehicle in full working order and with 50 gallons of water in the tank to only 4 tons 15 cwt, making the Steam Sapper the lightest traction engine ever built until that time in its power class. The vehicle was shod with rubber tyres in segment, on the main wheels, each sheathed in wrought iron strips and with angle iron strips between each segment. Thus the rubber formed a resilient 'sandwich' round the rims and any damaged segment could be easily replaced. The front wheels also had rubber segment tyres.

On the trials the Steam Sapper proved most satisfactory and towed a 15-ton train of three wagons over a course which included Star Hill, Chatham, where grades of 1 in 10 were negotiated with ease. Despite the 6-h.p. rating as much as 40 h.p. was recorded during tests.

Steam Sappers were duly ordered for the Royal Engineers and by 1873 nine were in service at Rochester and furnished virtually all the British Army's mechanical power at that time. One was fitted with a crane jib on the front to act as a travelling crane and all could be used for normal road haulage and for power driving of pumps and machinery. They could also be fitted with a drum on the main shaft to act as winding engines. Also provided were sets of special wide wheels which could be fitted as required in place of the normal road wheels to make the Steam Sapper into a light roller for road building. The most important optional fittings, however, were the flanged railway wheels, to 4 ft 8½ in. gauge, with which any of the Steam Sappers could be used as light railway locomotives. These were used on the 2½-mile military railway between Upnor and the Medway which was specially constructed to serve the ammunition and powder magazines near Upnor. Aveling and Porter built special wagons to go with the Steam Sappers and these also had alternative sets of road and railway wheels.

Towards the end of 1873 a military force was sent to the Gold Coast under General Sir Garnet Wolseley to seize Kumasi and put down the Ashanti. To accomplish this, however, it was found that a large military expedition was required. Long distances were involved on the proposed advance inland and Wolseley decided to build a railway, possibly as long as 50 miles, which would be used to supply the expeditionary force as it moved forward. Three of the Steam Sappers from Rochester were earmarked to provide the power and one was shipped out in pieces to Cape Coast. Quantities of track from the military railway at Upnor were also shipped out, together with some Aveling and Porter wagons and ten special wagons specially built to carry wounded; it was proposed that wounded men would be quickly transported back to Cape Coast from the firing line on the return journeys made by the Steam Sappers. In the event, however, these grandiose and far-sighted plans came to almost nothing. The land was quite unknown and unsurveyed, so tracklaying proved very slow and difficult. Little progress was made and the first run of the Steam Sapper ended after 2 miles when the vehicle overturned owing to the uneven nature of the tracks. It was taken back to Cape Coast Castle, the British headquarters, and there used as a stationary boiler to

provide power for sawing firewood. Later the floods came and what had been laid in the way of railroad was washed away.

Aveling and Porter also sold many Steam Sappers to foreign governments for military use, notably to Italy, France, and Russia. Six Steam Sappers were used by the Russians in the Russo-Turkish War of 1876–78 (together with six other assorted types) and collectively these Russian-owned vehicles hauled more than 9,000 tons of military stores during the course of the war. This was not the first time traction engines were actually used by military forces in wartime, for as early as 1870 British-built Fowler traction engines had been used by the German Army (see plate 5).

5   **Fowler Road Locomotive,** 1870, U.K./Germany.

The first occasion on which traction engines were actually used under war conditions was during the Siege of Paris in the Franco-Prussian War of 1870. The Prussian War Department had ordered eight Fowler traction engines in 1869 and the first two of these were delivered on 20 August 1870, when they arrived at Pont-à-Mousson. They were instantly put to work on general haulage work in support of the army. In their first five days of service they hauled a dozen stores wagons over the 45 kilometres from Pont-à-Mousson to Commercy. Later, in a seven day period, they transported 1,000 100 kg. crates of ammunition and 50 100 kg. crates of coal between Nanteuil and Villeneuve St. Georges after the destruction of the Nanteuil railway tunnel threatened to cut the German supply route. At the

Siege of Paris the vehicles became something of a legend and they were used to haul coal wagons, ammunition wagons, and, on occasion, guns. Quite apart from demonstrating the great value of mechanical transport in military operations, these Fowler engines also spurred on the French military authorities to take an interest in mechanical transport —for some years previously French army officers who had been advocating its use had been disregarded by the War Ministry.

The Fowlers used by the Germans were standard vehicles, not specially prepared for military service in any way. They weighed 40 tons and were of about 20 h.p.

6 Fowler Artillery Siege Train Traction Engine, 1880, U.K.

While many military vehicles were (and still are) adaptations of basically commercial designs, special types have been produced over the years exclusively for specific military roles. This vehicle built by John Fowler & Co. of Leeds, a major traction engine producer, was one of the first types actually designed by the military authorities, in this case for work with the heavy artillery. Responsible for its design was a Mr J. A. C. Hay who was chief of the machinery section of the British Ordnance Department. The requirement was for a versatile vehicle which could haul heavy guns, ammunition wagons or store wagons on road or rail, and also serve the guns and assist in mounting them. The road wheels illustrated could be replaced as required with flanged railway wheels to a 4 ft 8½ in. gauge. The prototype was actually completed late in 1879 and was subjected to a series of exhaustive tests which well illustrate the versatility of the design. At the Ordnance Department's proving ground at Shoeburyness it hauled a train of no less than 14 field guns (total weight 34 tons) over roads, fields, and marsh at an average speed of 4 m.p.h. It was then used to transfer the barrel of a 68-pdr. gun, by means of its front-mounted steam crane, from one road carriage to another. Next it was used to power the tackle of a gyn to lift a 12-ton gun from the ground. For this the whip of the tackle was taken round one of the power-driven capstans with which the vehicle was fitted, visible just behind the main wheel in the picture. With the vehicle stationary, a further test involved using the capstan to haul a train of guns (weight 10 tons) across country from a distance, while in a similar test a 38-ton gun and carriage were hauled from a barge across a beach and over a sea-wall with a 1 in. 16 sloped face. The performance of the Siege Train Engine was no less impressive in marshy conditions. It towed a 40-pdr. gun (weighing 4 tons) across boggy ground until the entire equipage was completely sunk to its axles and immobilised in the mud. Using a wire rope and the powered capstan, the vehicle hauled itself free after the rope had been passed round a suitable tree. Then it hauled the gun free and proceeded on its journey. Tested on its flanged wheels with buffers added front and rear, the vehicle then acted like a locomotive and towed a 38-ton gun and carriage up a 1 in 40 gradient as well as towing trains of ordinary rail wagons at up to 8 m.p.h. In final tests, of a more general nature, the vehicle was used to provide power for pumping and driving circular saws.

A vertical 'coffee pot' boiler was used to make room within the usual traction engine wheelbase for the crane and a big operating platform. The driving platform was between the crane and the boiler with a coal bunker on each side. Wood could be used instead of coal if necessary. The vehicle had single-cylinder drive and was of 8 h.p. (nominal). It weighed 12 tons in all and the crane was stressed for 5 tons. The main wheels were $6\frac{1}{2}$ ft in diameter.

The Fowler Siege Train Engine, as a purpose-built vehicle for artillery and engineer use in the field, was far ahead of its time; but it appeared at a quiet time in British military history and was relatively little used.

7 **Tracteur Scotte,** 1894–98, France.

After the Franco-Prussian war, the French War Ministry made some progress with examining possible future designs of steam tractor for military service. Seven traction engines were purchased in the 1870s, five of indigenous manufacture and two Steam Sappers (Plate 4). Various other vehicles were tried out over the years but the first practical steam tractor intended specifically for military use was designed and perfected by a M. Scotte of Epernay, a hatter by profession. In 1894 Scotte entered his vehicle for a race from Paris to Rouen which was organised by a leading French newspaper. Scotte's tractor did not win and he returned to Epernay to carry out improvements—it was said that the Mayor of Epernay made him fit bells to the vehicle to give warning of his approach since so many

citizens had been frightened by the noise. In 1897 the Automobile-Club de France organised what was to become an annual trial for road vehicles and the recently formed 'Commission Militaire des Automobiles' took an interest in this event since they were seeking suitable vehicles for possible military use. Seven vehicles entered the trials, among which was Scotte's 'tracteur' or 'camion à vapeur'. This vehicle impressed the Commission, particularly its director, an artillery colonel. The artillery hired the Scotte tractor for the summer of 1898 when they held trials at Versailles and the Scotte gave a distinguished performance, hauling guns weighing over 25 tons and 'trains' of up to nine wagons, each one normally drawn by a team of horses. In fact, the nine wagons represented the complete battery transport to accompany the gun. The Scotte tractor as it appeared at this time is shown with the legend 'Train Scotte' which was applied for the hauling trials. On a good road the Scotte could carry 4 tons on its load platform and tow up to 12 tons. It developed 27 h.p. and could travel 50 kilometres before refuelling with coal and water. The vehicle was very reliable and the Commission reported that for the first time they had tested a mechanical vehicle which was satisfactory for military service in every way and completely superior to animal transport. In cost, manpower, and the numbers needed the Tracteur Scotte was better on all counts than horse draught, and the Commission ended their report by formally requesting that six Scotte tractors be purchased for the artillery, each with five trailers. However, this request was rejected by the War Ministry on the grounds that the military budget would not justify the great expense and that, in any case, the roads generally were not as yet good enough for the Scotte tractor to operate freely all over the country. This latter was a somewhat lame excuse for the trials had taken the vehicle over all conditions of road surface without any great effect on performance. However, this very advanced vehicle was fated to see little military service; only two were purchased for the army and this was not until 1900, after a further set of trials.

8 McLaren 70-h.p. Traction Engine, 1899, U.K.

By the time of the South African War in 1899 the British Army had been using traction engines for some years. With the mobile fast-moving nature of the operations in South Africa, the use of traction engines in some numbers appealed to the British C-in-C, Lord Roberts. Several traction engines were taken to South Africa by Colonel Templer who commanded the Balloon Section of the Royal Engineers. These were to haul the balloon wagons. Subsequently Lord Roberts sent for Colonel R. Crompton, the man who had organised traction engine transport for the Indian Government (see Plate 3). Crompton was placed in overall charge of all Army traction engine transport in South Africa. A number of commercial traction engines were purchased second-hand in Britain for war service in South Africa, but some vehicles were also purchased new. Among these were McLaren 70-h.p. engines of this firm's standard 'Colonial' type, some of which had already been in service commercially in South Africa at work in the diamond

mines. The McLaren 70-h.p. traction engines were among the most powerful built and they had an extra large firebox and grate for wood burning, plus extra large water tanks which allowed them to travel up to 12 miles before replenishing. In addition the wheels were extra wide for travelling over soft ground, and there was a generous canopy to give protection from the sun. The front axle was steered by worm and rack, instead of the more usual chains, so as to give more positive steering on narrow roads, while the axles were carried on leaf springs, an advanced (but not exclusive) feature of McLaren designs. The engine was of the 'compound' type—that is the steam was passed successively through high pressure and low pressure cylinders to give increased power. The McLaren engine could haul loads of up to 55 tons up inclines as steep as 1 in 12.

A feature of the McLaren which specially commended it for military use was a portable 7-ton crane jib (not shown in the illustration) which could be bolted on the front each side of the smokebox. This crane could be erected in only a few minutes since it was attached by only four bolts, two at the feet of the jib arms and two to secure the backstays. The crane was worked by worm wheel gear.

In addition to traction engines, Mc-Laren also supplied the War Department with so-called 'traction wagons' for stores carrying. These resembled railway box-vans except that they were on iron road wheels and were intended to be hauled by the traction engines. Using its portable crane, the McLaren engine could actually lift and carry one of the traction wagons bodily. The McLaren engines and wagons were the most important types ordered for Army use at this period and Mr W. A. McLaren, younger brother of the two partners in the firm (J. & H. McLaren of Leeds) actually went out to South Africa to serve as an adviser on their use to the Army's Director of Traction Engine Transport.

Another important type of traction engine used by the Army in South Africa was the Fowler, and some of these had the distinction of being among the first armoured vehicles used anywhere on active service. They had a box-like armoured superstructure added and towed armoured wagons specially built to carry 4.7-inch howitzers (on field carriages) and ammunition. They were built for defensive rather than offensive purposes, however, the idea being to provide immunity from the Boer commandos which used to attack the British transport column. Details of the Fowler armoured traction engines are outside the scope of this book, however. In 1902, largely as a result of the success of traction engines in South Africa, the firm of Fowler built a new series of vehicles for the British Army which could burn coal, wood, or oil and could haul up to 60 tons. The design of these Fowler vehicles was very similar to the original 1870 design shown in Plate 5.

9   **Keller Tractor,** 1900, Germany.

This novel vehicle was an early attempt to provide four-wheel drive and cross-country ability by an ingenious 'wheels-within-wheels' system. The work of a German inventor named Keller, it was tested by both the German and British War Departments, but in neither case was it adopted for service. Essentially this was a tram type of vehicle fitted with its own continuous tracks. It was powered by a 20-b.h.p. Capitaine oil engine mounted between the rear pair of wheels with the gearbox in the centre of the vehicle. The small sprung road wheels were 2 ft 2 in. in diameter and were driven by belts from the transmission. These belts are visible beneath the chassis. The wheels ran inside free-moving road rail rings $7\frac{1}{2}$ ft in diameter, with troughs $6\frac{1}{2}$ inches wide. These road rails were held in place by two small guide rollers which were sprung horizontally and attached to the interior framing of the body. When the wheel ran over an obstacle, like a rock, the road rail was slowed up as it lifted vertically; but it was forced against the spring of the guide rollers and the road wheels so that the upward movement was considerably dampened and the road rail returned to its normal position with very little displacement as the vehicle passed completely over the obstacle. In effect the damping was not unlike that afforded by a pneumatic tyre. The body and chassis framing of the vehicle was actually in two halves, pivoted vertically at the centre and allowing an up-and-down motion to match, within limits of the contours of the ground. Each pair of guide rollers (not visible in the drawing but actually sited across the horizontal diameter of the road rails) was linked with the opposite pair on the other road rail by means of a cross-girder. The driver steered by 'tiller' levers which acted on the cross-girder and turned the linked guide rollers, and thus the road rails, to right or left as required. Steering and controls were duplicated at each end. The vehicle was 25 ft long, 7 ft wide, and 10 ft high.

It had two gears which gave speeds of 2½ m.p.h. and 4.9 m.p.h. Total weight was 5 tons. Tests with the vehicle over logs, sandy soil, and wet macadam were most impressive, with the tractor towing a train of wagons loaded to 55 tons.

An Englishman, Mr Charles Crowden of Leamington, obtained the British agency for this vehicle and arranged a six-day trial for the British War Department at Aldershot. Though the War Department spent 18 months considering its findings and also sent officers to Germany to make further enquiries, they did not in the event order this vehicle for service. Apart from its four-wheel drive capability, a major advantage claimed by the inventor was its cheapness to run compared with normal steam traction engines.

10 **Renault Car,** 1900–01, France.

The French Army was one of the first to make extensive use of the petrol engine, as opposed to steam traction, which was not surprising in view of France's pre-eminence at the time in the development of the motor car. At the major French motor show in 1900—the Exposition Universelle—there were no less than eleven different vehicles displayed which had been developed specially for military use. These included a De Dion-Bouton tricar for liaison work, Decauville and Mors staff cars, a Panhard et Levassor bus adapted as a troop transport, a De Dietrich medical van, a Sautter telegraph wagon and van, a pigeon van, a military post office van, a Scotte tractor (Plate 6), and, finally, a De Dion-Bouton steam lorry. Examples of most of these types were purchased by the French War Department and were used in the annual military manoeuvres at Beauce in that year. A total of 35,000 francs was included in the military budget of 1900 for the purchase of these vehicles. Additionally in return for an indemnity, reserve officers used their own cars. Another vehicle which was used and gained much publicity on account of its novelty was a Renault 4½-h.p. car which was fitted at the rear with a dynamo. When the car was stationary the motor could be run to charge the dynamo which in turn powered an electric searchlight used for signalling at ranges of 2 to 3 kilometres. The Renault was a perfectly standard production car of the time apart from the added dynamo. It had a De Dion engine and a top speed of about 12 m.p.h.

11 **Thornycroft Steam Wagon (Types A and B),** 1901, U.K.

In 1900 following the demonstration of the usefulness of mechanical transport in the South African War, the British War Office set up a Mechanical Transport Committee to establish future requirements and procure suitable designs. In December 1901, the Committee held trials at Aldershot in a prize competition for 'self-propelled lorries for military purposes'. When the competition was first announced, eleven entries were submitted, but only five were actually presented for tests. Two vehicles were steam lorries submitted by Thornycroft, one was a Straker steam lorry, one was a Foden steam lorry, and the other was a Milnes-Daimler motor lorry. Total prizes of £850 were offered for the best three designs. The Thornycroft vehicles were of two different types. The Type A was the standard commercial product with a payload of 3 tons and could haul a load of up to 2 tons on a trailer. It had its boiler and driving controls at the front end. The second vehicle, the Type B, was specially developed for military purposes and had several important changes. To make it more suitable for working over rough ground it had larger wheels than the Type A and stronger springs with increased tilt angle for the front axles. The boiler and mechanical arrangements were as for the Type A except that the layout was reversed with boiler and driving position over the rear wheels in order to give better traction. Another special feature was the provision of a three-speed winding drum and 100 yards of wire rope. Drive was on the 'compound' principle and one man could both steer and drive the vehicle. Steering was by worm-gearing and there was a steam brake. The bunkers allowed fuel for up to 50 miles and coal or oil fuel could be used. This vehicle weighed $6\frac{1}{2}$ tons. Both the Type A and Type B vehicles are shown.

The trials were held in the environs of Aldershot during a single week with different routes in different conditions each day. One test involved climbing the not inconsiderable gradient of the road over the Hog's Back at Hindhead. Of all the entries, the Milnes-Daimler motor lorry was the least successful and broke down several times. The Straker steam lorry was the least successful of the steam entrants and the top prize of £500 went to the Thornycroft Type A lorry (ironically enough the 'standard' vehicle, not the special 'militarised' Type B) while the second prize of £250 went to the Foden steam lorry, with the

Straker as runner-up. The War Office purchased the Thornycroft Type A and Foden lorries and they became the earliest types of mechanised load carriers in British Army service.

12 **Sautter Harlé Pigeon Van,** 1900–01, France.

Another type shown at the Exposition Universelle in 1900 was a vehicle specially constructed for the transport of carrier pigeons by the firm of Sautter Harlé et Cie. This was a purely speculative adaptation by the builders of a standard petrol truck they were selling commercially. Apart from its paint finish and the racks to hold the pigeon cages there was nothing of significance about it. It was demonstrated to the French Army but there is no record of its being taken into service. However, this pigeon van is a good example of a very early design for specialised military requirements and the same exhibition included a telegraph-line-laying wagon by the same maker. The Sautter Harlé had a Koch horizontal petrol engine mounted under the driver's seat with the usual chain drive of the period to the rear wheels.

13 **Davidson's Duryea Machine-Gun Car,** 1899, U.S.A.

Meanwhile, across the Atlantic, a military officer of the Illinois National Guard, Major R. P. Davidson, became one of the first to appreciate how mechanical transport could be utilised in a highly mobile offensive role. In 1899 he obtained a standard 6-h.p. Duryea tricar and altered it to take a Colt 7-mm. machine-gun complete with its tripod which was affixed to the front platform of the vehicle with its front legs straddling the single front wheel. The gun had a light shield and could be traversed by hand through 180° and also had limited vertical movement. The range of the gun was 2,000 yards and it could fire 480 rounds per minute, by belt feed. A crew of four men, in pairs back to back, could be carried on the standard passenger seats which were placed over the engine cover. The Duryea tricar had a three-cylinder engine and weighed 900 lbs without, and 1,000 lbs with, the gun. A rope was carried on the vehicle so that the engine could be used as a winch to haul the vehicle out of mud so long as there was a handy tree or fence, etc., to take the rope. When fully loaded the vehicle could carry tents for the men and 5000 rounds of ammunition. Davidson was an instructor at the North West Military Academy and he envisaged using the tricar as the main vehicle of a 'flying artillery' patrol with an escort of armed cyclists.

In 1900 Davidson produced an almost exactly similar vehicle, this time based on a Duryea quadricycle which was like the tricar except that it had two front wheels instead of one. This is the vehicle illustrated. In the summer of 1900, Davidson took this car from Fort Sheridan, Illinois, to Washington with a crew of Academy cadets, to deliver a message from his local commander to the U.S. Army Chief of Staff, General Nelson A. Miles. This very convincing display of the military value of fast (for its day) motor transport impressed General Miles, and as a result he later (in 1903) suggested to the Secretary of State for War that five existing cavalry regiments should be equipped with Davidson's cars as an 'automobile corps' for patrol, reconnaissance, road marking, and military survey. However nothing came of this far-sighted idea and it was many years before any nation organised this type of force.

In England in late 1899, a young Anglo-American motor engineer, F. R. Simms, had demonstrated a machine-gun-armed De Dion-Bouton quadricycle very similar to that evolved by Davidson, but this was a one-man machine, less practical than Davidson's design, and it was never actually put to any military use.

14 **Davidson's Steam Machine-Gun Car,** 1902, U.S.A.

Though the military authorities did not appreciate the full potential of Davidson's or General Miles' ideas, Davidson himself carried on his pioneering work in the use of mechanical transport. At the North West Military Academy, Davidson formed a new machine-gun patrol in 1902, this time using the Colt machine-gun mounted on two steam cars built by the pupils under his command. The steam car formed a more sturdy carriage than the quadricycle. The first vehicle was demonstrated at a motor show held in St. Louis, but still the U.S. War Department showed no interest in this kind of equipment. However, publicity from the exhibition led to other nations making similar adaptations to commercial vehicles. In Britain in 1905, for instance, the War Office modified a saloon car to take a Maxim machine-gun, complete with gunner, in the front seat alongside the driver. The gun pointed out through the windscreen. A few more cars were subsequently purchased and similarly modified with a view to using them for police work in the colonies. Meanwhile the Admiralty toyed with the idea of embarking one or two on ships for the use of naval landing parties. The illustration shows Davidson's historic vehicle, one of the first to mount a gun.

15 Cadillac Balloon Destroyer, 1908–10, U.S.A.

Davidson continued to refine his original ideas. In 1909 he purchased a Cadillac car and fitted it with a Colt machine-gun on a tripod mount to make yet another machine-gun car. Like some military men of other nations, Davidson had realised early on that operations on land were now facing the threat of observation—if not attack—from the air. The observation balloon and airship had been perfected and Davidson was one of the first to appreciate that a gun mounted on a fast car was a quick way of catching up with and eliminating any intruders in the sky. So in 1910 Davidson bought two more Cadillacs and converted them to 'Balloon Destroyers' with two Colt machine-guns mounted on each vehicle. One, with a shield, was on the scuttle and the other was at the rear.

To demonstrate the mobility of these Balloon Destroyers, Davidson entered both in the famous Glidden Tour of 1910, a severe long distance run from Cleveland to Chicago via Mississippi and Texas. Only 9 out of 38 cars finished, among them the two balloon destroyers which had been crewed by some of Davidson's cadets.

Davidson, later a Colonel, went on to play a prominent part in the early

development of American armoured cars, but this is beyond the scope of this book.

16 Straker-Squire Motor Ambulance Van, 1906–08, U.K.

The British Army carried out further trials of mechanised vehicles in 1903 and in the same year the first Motor Transport Company was formed under the aegis of the Army Service Corps, who were made responsible for the future procurement and organisation of motor vehicles. A variety of vehicles were acquired or taken in charge including the existing steam lorries and traction engines. Cars and motor lorries were also purchased. The vehicle shown here is the very first motor ambulance used by the British Army, which was taken into service in 1906. It was first used 'in the field' in the summer manoeuvres of 1907 when it was attached to a military hospital in Oxford and operated between there and the big military camps set up at Thame and Aylesbury for the duration of the exercises. Contemporary photographs show it attracting much attention as it overtakes the marching troops.

17 Milnes-Daimler Motor Wagon, 1906–08, U.K.

A contemporary type in service with the Straker-Squire ambulance, the Milnes-Daimler was built by the Milnes company from chassis and mechanical components imported from the German Daimler company. The original Milnes-Daimler of 1901 was one of the first motor lorries in Britain, and one took part (though dogged with mechanical troubles) in the War Office trials held in Aldershot that year. By 1906 several 20-h.p. Milnes-Daimlers were in service with the M.T. Company of the Army Service Corps at Aldershot, and they too took part in the 1907 manoeuvres. The Milnes-Daimler was one of the best available chassis of the day with several advanced features. Unusual on a motor lorry was the screw brake for the rear wheels, which can be seen adjacent to the steering wheel. The vehicle had four speeds plus reverse with two gear levers each controlling two speeds. The single cone clutch automatically disengaged when the gear levers were moved though there was also a clutch pedal. Drive was by carden shaft and the final drive was via geared drums bolted to the inside of the rear wheel hubs, giving a somewhat noisy ride.

18 Hannoversche Maschinenbau Steam Lorry, 1908, Germany

This was one of the first lorries to be used by the German Army and first attracted attention at the Berlin Motor Show in November 1906. Early in 1907 some were acquired for service after initial testing by the Army Transport Service. The drawing shows the first vehicle still in its maker's finish. The Hannoversche Maschinenbau lorry was a 4-ton vehicle of 20–25-h.p. fitted with a Stolz vertical boiler. It was fitted with Krupp's patent wheels which had cast-steel hubs and spokes shod with rubber 'tyres' over which steel tyres were shrunk into place. This gave a wheel with a resilient rubber insert which economised on rubber and was hard wearing; it is interesting to note that the Germans again developed wheels of

this sort on tanks late in World War 2, when rubber became extremely scarce. The Hannoversche Maschinenbau lorry was a good load hauler. On Army trials it carried 5 tons and towed a trailer with $1\frac{1}{2}$ tons over a course which included 1 in 10 slopes. Average speed was 6 m.p.h.

19 Train Renard, 1904, France

In the early 1900s the French military authorities purchased a number of vehicles of various sorts and attempts were made to find the best designs for military service. For colonial service a few more Scotte tractors were purchased in 1904, but a new vehicle appeared which was designed by a serving engineer officer, Colonel Renard in an attempt to overcome the limitations of a normal vehicle towing a train of dumb wagons. One of these limitations was that the vehicle was towing a dead weight so the actual length of the tow depended on the vehicle's adhesion; secondly there was no control over the tow, either for braking or steering, which made manoeuvring difficult.

Renard's idea was to fit up a petrol tractor with carden shaft transmission and a rear extension from the drive shaft. He proposed to adapt a train of wagons so that each would have a shaft and differential with a matching rear extension. The ends of the drive shafts were articulated. Under the Renard system, all the shafts were joined up to the rear drive shaft of the tractor so that there was a continuous flexible drive to all wagons in the train. Only the respective rear axles of the trailers were driven, the front axles pivoting in the usual way. With Renard's system a smaller tractor could haul a larger load, and there would be almost complete control over braking and steering. The illustration shows the prototype tractor —which was in fact a converted 50-h.p. car—with the rear extension of the drive shaft clearly visible. Chains and a weighted chassis were used to give maximum traction. The conversion work was carried out by the firm of Surcouf in 1904 and on trials the Renard tractor hauled a 36-ton train of trailers at speeds from 16 to 72 km.p.h. This was sufficiently impressive for three more vehicles and three complete trains (each of three wagons) to be ordered. These were first used in the summer manoeuvres of 1907 in the hands of the Service de l'Intendance. However, though the idea was ingenious it was also complicated. It took a minimum of 20 minutes to join up the shafts for the road and any sharp turns meant that they had to be disconnected. Similarly there was the cost of converting or building special wagons and it was concluded that ordinary lorries were, in the long run, more convenient to operate than Renard trains. Thus no more Renard outfits were ordered, though the German Army was interested in the idea and converted three Daimler trucks and wagons on a similar principle for service in South West Africa. Italian and American firms also experimented on the same lines.

20 Genty's Panhard Automitrailleuse, 1908, France

Captain Genty was a French artillery officer who had joined the army in 1886. Always mechanically-minded, he became an enthusiastic motorist in his spare time from the moment cars first

appeared in the 1890s and became a self-taught motor engineer from servicing his own car. He took part in several early motor rallies and races, and because of his interest in the subject he was included among the committee of army officers sent to the 1900 Exposition Universelle to report on vehicles likely to be of military value, particulary heavy lorries. His report pleased the War Ministry and he was sent to lecture the Staff Course on the military use of cars. Subsequently Genty was placed in charge of the General Staff's staff cars, and then, in mid-1901, took charge of the workshop company at Vincennes and became responsible for motor car maintenance. In 1903 this company became the nucleus of a 'corps d'automobilistes militarie'. All the while Genty's fame as a racing motorist was spreading. For the 1903 manoeuvres Genty commanded an 'automobile company' made of reserve officers who provided their own cars. In 1904 and 1905 Genty was Chief of Staff of the 1st Cavalry Division and drove an army Panhard et Levassor car which he used with great dash and skill for reconnaissance and patrol work on manoeuvres. This experience made him realise the potential military value of a car carrying armament, and after the 1905 manoeuvres he was given permission to fix a machine-gun to his 1904 Panhard. As modified the car was given a pintle on the rear to take a Hotchkiss machine-gun and a column with pintle between the two front seats. The front passenger seat was modified to revolve so that the gunner could sit in it and fire to the rear when necessary. In its machine-gun-carrier role the Panhard had a crew of four, carried 500 rounds of ammunition and had a top speed of 45 km.p.h.

In the autumn manoeuvres of 1906 there was a chance to compare Genty's car with a new Charron armoured car which had just been built. Though Genty's car was unarmoured it won high praise for efficiency, simplicity and versatility from the generals. The Charron armoured car, on the other hand was criticised because it soon became unbearably hot inside the armoured body and it was not considered to be well enough armed. A testing commission of generals were enthusiastic enough about Genty's car to commend the adoption of this type of 'auto mitrailleuse' on the scale of two cars per cavalry brigade in the event of hostilities. The General Staff, however, took no action on this suggestion. Events spurred them on, for in 1907 there was an uprising of dissident tribesmen in Casablanca and an expeditionary force was sent from France to restore order. Operations dragged on with long desert frontiers to patrol and General Lyautey, the local commander, remembered Genty's car and asked that it (and Genty) be sent over to help in patrol work for which conditions it seemed ideal. Genty arrived on 18 December and between then and the beginning of February 1908, he and his now ageing car covered over 4,000 kilometres on patrol, reconnaissance and liaison work. Decorated for his services, Genty asked for two identical cars to be purchased and equipped. No official authority was forthcoming for ordering Panhards however, so Genty arranged to get two Clement-Bayards, with similar bodywork to the Panhard. These subsequently proved to be a bad buy, being too heavy, too noisy, too long, and difficult to drive.

Meanwhile Genty crashed his own Panhard into a ravine while on desert patrol, was badly injured and repatriated to France. He had demonstrated by this time how valuable his military car was, especially in desert conditions, and two new cars identical to his own were now ordered. Genty retired soon in poor health from a combination of his injuries and exhaustion from his desert work. He died in 1916. Though hardly remembered now, Genty was one of the first to demonstrate the value of the light car in desert conditions and in actual combat.

21 Armstrong-Whitworth Military Transport Wagon, 1908, U.K.

This was a very early example of a motor lorry designed and built specifically for military purposes by Sir W. G. Armstrong-Whitworth & Co. Ltd. of Newcastle-on-Tyne, the prominent arms manufacturers, who produced a prototype early in 1908. A unique feature was the multi-purpose body which enabled it to be used as a troop carrier, a load carrier, or a combination of the two. As a troop carrier it had five transverse 'garden seats' which accommodated a total of 25 men. Each seat—and the driving compartment bulkhead—had leather clips on the back which held the mens' rifles. There was a further seat for an officer or an N.C.O. alongside the driver and this had a folding mapboard attached to the front scuttle.

To convert the vehicle to a load carrier, the seats were unbolted from their transverse positions, folded down to form side sections, and bolted on to the end of the flatbed platform. One seat formed the tailgate and the other four formed the sides. By leaving the two seats *in situ*, 10 men could be carried while the rear half of the body was still given over to cargo. An ammunition locker was fitted each side at the rear beneath the flatbed body, each locker holding 4,000 rounds of rifle ammunition. There was a toolbox under the body at the rear. A running board was fitted each side to facilitate embarkation.

The vehicle was 7 ft wide and 21 ft 3 in. long, with a wheelbase of 13 ft 6 in. It had a four-cylinder 40-h.p. engine with four speeds and reverse, and chain drive. Top speed was about 12 m.p.h. and there were twin rear wheels. Chassis was a 3-ton Maudslay. This vehicle was a 'private venture' design which, though tested by the British Army, was not adopted. The Army did adopt the Maudslay lorry at this time, however, following an impressive display by one of these lorries at the 1907 R.A.C. Trials. The Maudslays ordered for service, however, had only plain load-carrying bodies with slatted floors. Dimensionally and in appearance they were similar to the Armstrong-Whitworth lorry in its load-carrying form, though the slats were more widely spaced.

It is interesting to note that a similar troop carrying idea was tried in America in 1910 when a Major Hugh Gallagher designed a vehicle with seats for 16 soldiers. Two seats only were fitted, running the length of the body back to back, with a water tank between them and a ration locker at the rear. This provided sustenance for the men on patrols of several days' duration. Gallagher

converted a White 2-ton lorry with this equipment and arranged a trial run for the War Department when 16 troops and an officer were taken on an 11-hour, 264-mile run from Atlanta to Fort Oglethorpe and back. However, no further progress was made with the idea as the U.S. Army lacked the money to buy vehicles of this type.

22 **Adler 25-cwt Light Lorry,** 1908, Germany

The first use of motor transport on an organised basis in the German Army took place in the Summer manoeuvres of 1908 when a 'commissariat train' of four Adler 25-cwt light lorries was attached to the 25th Cavalry Brigade (The Grand Ducal Hessian). Until this time it had been the practice in the German Army for the Commissariat Department to hire (or otherwise requisition) suitable carts and horses for supply work locally. Similarly, forage for horses and provisions for troops were purchased from local sources wherever the army happened to be deployed. Under the new system of mechanisation, food and store depots were set up at Frankfurt and Hanon. The lorries carried supplies from these bases to the exercise areas in the Westphalian district. The four lorries made the return journey of over 100 miles daily. These Adlers were simply commercial vehicles purchased and suitably painted for military use. They each carried a driver and a Commissariat N.C.O.

Experience in the Summer manoeuvres was so successful that no less than six heavy lorries were put into service for the 18th Army Corps in the Autumn manoeuvres of September

1908. The lorries operated between Lahn and Sieg and each towed one or more trailers; these were vehicles of the old horse-drawn type with drawbars modified to fit the lorries. Some of these vehicles were of the steam type, but at least one was a Siemens and Schukert petrol-electric tractor.

23 Northover/Harley-Davidson Machine-Gun Carrier, 1908, Canada

The use of the motor cycle for military despatch riders dates from the turn of the century. One of the first recorded instances of a motor cycle being armed for patrol and reconnaissance was a Harley-Davidson machine which was converted by a Sergeant Northover of the Canadian Militia in 1908. He fixed a modified sidecar to his machine and mounted a standard Maxim machine-gun arranged to fire to the front. Northover was an armourer who made some important contributions to machine-gun development in his own right. This was a non-official idea which Northover demonstrated on manoeuvres. However, most armies later adopted this idea and motor cycle machine-gun combinations were widely used by all the major nations in both world wars. Later examples are shown in this book.

24 Thornycroft 50-h.p. Heavy Oil Engine Tractor, 1909, U.K.

In July 1908, the British War Office announced a competition for light military tractors, and set up a Mechanical Transport Committee of senior officers under the Director of Transport and Remounts—the equine influence was still considerable—whose duty it was to organise trials and selection. Apart from finding suitable vehicles for military use, it was thought that standards could be established which would give vehicle manufacturers a good basis for comparison when qualifying for participation in a newly organised War Office subsidy scheme.

The conditions for competitors were exacting. The trials were to take place at the end of February 1909, just 6 months later (so as to fall within the financial year, not to test the speed of construction), and there was no limit to the number of entries from each manufacturer. The War Office undertook to buy the winning design and any promising types of good enough standard. Weight limit was 7 tons gross with fuel for 100-miles and 6 tons tare. The vehicle also had to be capable of towing an 8-ton load over this distance and up a grade of 1 in 10. Speed range was to be within $1\frac{1}{2}$–7 m.p.h. and the vehicle had to be capable of wading to 2 ft unprepared and have some cross-country ability. It had to be sprung, have two brake systems, be fitted with an awning, be capable of one-man drive, and have a winding drum or winch with 100 yards of wire rope tested to 7 tons. The competition was to be judged on overall fuel cost, performance over a set course, ease of maintenance, and general mechanical efficiency.

Eleven vehicles were entered, but only three of them were actually ready inside the time limit and only these competed. The trials' took place in the first ten days of March 1909, during a particularly severe spell of winter weather. This much increased the difficulties of the competitors in the series of test runs over seven different routes in the Farnborough—Long Valley—Aldershot districts. Included were hill climbs over the Hog's Back and other local steep gradients, speed trials and cross-country sections, with winching and towing tasks at all stages.

The outright winner of the three was Thornycroft's entry of a 50-h.p. oil engine (i.e. diesel) tractor. Awarded £750 first prize, Thornycroft sold the vehicle to the Army for £975. Thornycroft thus repeated their success of 1901 (Plate 11), but this time their vehicle was radically different. It had a four-cylinder oil engine at the front driving a cross shaft through level gear. From this a second shaft was driven by spur gear and this gave three speeds, including direct drive in top. The engine cylinders were cast in pairs and the power unit gave 40 b.h.p. at 700 r.p.m. running on paraffin. High- and low-tension magnetos were fitted and petrol could be used instead of paraffin if desired. A water tank was carried over the bonnet and there was a radiator at the front. There were two 45-gallon fuel tanks, one behind the driving seat and one behind the bonnet. The chassis was a simple structure of vertical steel plates with holes for axles, etc. The sliding pinion gears were so arranged that a winding drum on the right side of the chassis could be clutched in as desired. Traction engine wheels were fitted, with worm-gear steering at the front and 'grass hopper' leaf springs at the rear. The main wheels were 5 ft 8 in. diameter, 12 in. wide. Of the three competitors the Thornycroft's superiority was never in doubt. Apart from a veteran skilled driver, the Thornycroft had the best traction characteristics and a conveniently placed winding drum (un-

like its competitors). Thus the drum and a rope could be used instantly, controlled by the driver, to assist the vehicle over the steep icy grades on which the other vehicles faltered. Overall the Thornycroft had by far the lowest aggregate of unscheduled stops from breakdown and the highest overall average speed. One particular test involved crossing a bog, then using the winding drum to haul across a wagon. Only the Thornycroft surmounted this test completely. Defects were minor by contrast with the others tested, and the success of the Thornycroft was assured. The vehicle fully earned the Mechanical Transport Committee's prize and report 'that the machine presented by John I. Thornycroft and Company Limited is a great advance on anything previously offered for long-distance road haulage work for military purposes'.

25 **Broom & Wade 25-h.p. Military Tractor,** 1909, U.K.

Built by Messrs. Broom & Wade of High Wycombe, this vehicle was an unsuccessful contender in the War Office competition won by Thornycroft. It makes an interesting contrast to the Thornycroft design, however, and received a very favourable report from some members of the Mechanical Transport Committee. Like the Thornycroft tractor it had a simple steel channel chassis but it exhibited features in some ways more advanced. The front wheels had Ackermann-type steering from a conventional steering wheel while the front-wheel springs were not attached to the chassis but to a transverse spring. This gave a greatly superior ride. Best possible utilisation of chassis length was made, firstly by the 'forward control' position, and, secondly, by fitting the engine beneath the chassis. This was a single-cylinder paraffin unit which could also run on crude oils. The one large cylinder was $8\frac{1}{2}$ inches in diameter, and the very high compression meant that a considerable amount of water vapour had to be admitted with the air to prevent pre-ignition. Petrol or a blow-lamp were used for starting and a patent type of vaporiser was used to maintain combustion. The paraffin and petrol tanks were under the driving seat. The gear wheels were enclosed in an oil-tight box; they were in constant mesh and actuated by a solid clutch with spring drive. There were three forward speeds (of 7, 3 and 2 m.p.h.) plus reverse. The rear wheels were driven by gear rings, but the left hand ring was arranged to drive a winding drum which was located on the left of the chassis. The gear ring could, accordingly, be locked in or out with a moveable pin depending on whether or not the vehicle was stationary or moving. The Broom & Wade tractor was 12 ft 2 in. long, 7 ft wide, and had a wheelbase of 8 ft 5 in. The rear wheels were $5\frac{1}{2}$ ft in diameter and the front wheels 4 ft in diameter. On the trials the Broom & Wade vehicle impressed observers by its cross-country performance and the ease with which it winched its trailer over marshy ground. Speed and general performance, however, fell below the standard required as the 8-ton load which the test vehicles were required to handle was too much for the single-cylinder 25-h.p. engine. Compared to the Thornycroft tractor's £975 however, the Broom & Wade cost £495. Given a 5- or 6- instead of an 8-ton pay-load, it was generally thought to be a 'better buy' and more practical as it could also carry a payload itself which meant that its commercial (as against military) potential was greater than that of the Thornycroft. However, no military order for the Broom & Wade was given. The third tractor in the same trials was a steam-propelled vehicle by Stewart which was similar in size and layout to the Thornycroft machine. However, it ran a poor third to the Thornycroft and Broom & Wade vehicles throughout the trials.

26 **Milnes–Daimler Omnibus (Vanguard)**, 1908–09, U.K.
and
27 **Napier Light Lorry**, 1908–09, U.K.

The use of lorries for transporting stores and troops in Germany in the Summer and Autumn manoeuvres of 1908 inspired similar ideas in Britain. In December 1908 the secretary of the Mechanical Transport Committee, Captain R. K. Bagnall-Wild, organised a mobility exercise to test the feasibility of hiring commercial motor buses as troop transports in the event of an emergency. It was supposed that an enemy landing had taken place in the Thames estuary near Shoeburyness and that troops were to be rushed from London to defend the area. At short notice twenty-four buses and three service vehicles were hired from the London General Omnibus Co. and subsidiary companies (eight L.G.O.C. de Dions, eight Vanguard Milnes-Daimlers, and eight Road Cars Co. Straker-Squires were the buses involved). Two of these vehicles were used to simulate motor ambulances, and one was fitted as a staff vehicle for officers. The buses left their London garages at 5.30 a.m. and drove to Warley in Essex where they picked up 500 troops of the Territorial Army. In cold misty weather on the shortest day of the year, 21 December, the vehicles set off in two columns over two different routes with motor-cycle scouts riding ahead of each column and officers and official observers following up in cars. A Maxim machine-gun was mounted on the top deck of each leading bus. At Hadleigh in Essex the 'enemy' were sighted and the troops were deployed from the buses to the attack. This exercise proved to be highly successful and highly prophetic as well, for in 1914 when lorries were still in short supply London buses were requisitioned in an exactly similar way and sent to carry troops on the Western Front in the darkest days of the German advance into Flanders. A lesson learned from this early exercise in troop movement was the need for attendant breakdown vehicles in each column and the provision of spare vehicles where possible to make up numbers when breakdowns occurred. The illustration shows one of the Milnes-Daimlers with the Maxim machine crew on the top deck.

On 17 March 1909, a second and more ambitious demonstration of the value of motor transport took place, this time on a grander scale and involving regular troops. Because it was commercially sponsored, this second transport exercise was well-publicised at the time and is one of the best known landmarks in the history of military mechanisation. The Automobile Association initiated the idea and took up a suggestion of the Lincolnshire Automobile Club that in the event of war all its members should voluntarily hand their cars over to the government. For the 'experiment in mechanical transport' as the Automobile Association called it, the War Office were asked to suggest a coastal town where an invasion could be supposed to have taken place, the A.A. undertaking to provide the vehicles and organisation to move a battalion of troops to the area. A total of 411 vehicles was assembled consisting of 286 private cars, 21 Napier light lorries, five De Dion 40-h.p. lorries (borrowed from the L.G.O.C.), three Fiat lorries, and a Commer travelling workshop. A further 55 private cars (in which press representatives travelled) and 40 others (for War Office observers) made up the number. The troops totalled 1,000 and were drawn from the Coldstream, Grenadier, and Scots Guards. The soldiers were distributed amongst the cars and their 30 tons of stores were carried in the assortment of lorries. Split between three starting points, Chelsea Barracks, Wellington Barracks, and the Tower of London, the columns joined up at Crystal Palace at 10 a.m. and set off for the chosen venue, Hastings, some 70 miles away. First arrivals reached Hastings soon after 1 a.m. and the Guards were deployed on the seafront shortly afterwards.

Of the vehicles taking part, the 21 Napier light lorries, supplied by W. & G. Ducros Ltd. of Acton, were standard commercial four-cylinder vehicles, all with platform bodies and with uniformed drivers. Impeccably turned out, they created a good impression among the observers. Due to their good speed, the Napier lorries accompanied the cars and carried the support equipment which included ammunition, entrenching tools, first aid stores, and machineguns. Some towed water carts as well. The other lorries travelled in a separate convoy with bedding and provisions. A feature of the run was the Commer travelling workshop which was effective in repairing vehicles which broke down *en route*.

The London-Hastings run was much more of a stunt than the exercise with buses the previous December. The magazine *Commercial Motor* thought that the entire operation would have been swifter and better organised if buses and lorries had been used to carry the troops rather than the motley collection of cars which took part. It wondered whether anything likely to be really useful in case of war was definitely proved. In fact the run was really better publicity for the Automobile Association than the idea of moving troops big distances by road, but the point was successfully made that motor transport could speed up military operations far beyond the best ability of horse-drawn transport.

One of the 21 Napiers is shown; though not strictly a military vehicle, very similar 30-cwt Napiers with W.D. bodies were taken into service in large numbers a few years later, when the British Army was mechanised on a large scale.

28 Erhardt Balloon Destroyer, 1906, Germany

The very first vehicle with a gun intended for use against aerial targets was an Ehrhardt car which was modified by the German firm of Rheinmetall, Düsseldorf, in 1906 to mount one of the high

angle 5-cm., 30 calibre guns which had just been developed by that company. The vehicle was actually produced to demonstrate the potential of the weapon rather than to meet existing military requirements. The gun was hand-elevated and traversed from a pedestal which was fixed to the floor in the back of the vehicle. It had a maximum elevation of 70° and a depression of 5° with all-round traverse. To go with the gun, Rheinmetall produced a composite shrapnel shell known as the 'Brizanz Shell'. This projectile consisted of two parts; the lower two thirds were filled with shrapnel and exploded in the air working from a time fuse. The remaining third continued in flight until impact, trailing smoke to give a visual indication of the trajectory to the gunners. The Erhardt Balloon Destroyer had a crew of five and its total weight was 3,200 kg. It had a 50–60-h.p. engine, a top speed of 45 km.p.h., and could climb a 22° slope. Rheinmetall offered the car in its unarmoured form, as illustrated, or with an armoured body utilising 3·5 mm. nickel-steel plates and a gun shield. In this form the vehicle was one of the first German armoured cars though at the time it was described less dramatically as a 'protected car'. With the box-like armoured body in place, the mudguards were omitted. The Ehrhardt did not see formal military service though it was demonstrated to the military authorities.

29 Krupp-Daimler Balloon Destroyer (7·5 cm. gun), 1909, Germany

The great German firm of Krupp was instrumental in developing a gun with high elevation for use against airships and aircraft, an idea not necessarily originated but certainly perfected by them. Germany had by 1909 produced the Zeppelin, the best airship in the world at that time, and the military potential of the fast-developing aeroplane had been demonstrated. In addition tethered balloons were in wide military use for observation purposes. Krupp set out to produce a gun which was able to hit an airship at a height of at least 1½ miles with an angle of elevation of up to 75°. They modified three guns of different calibre, a 6·5 cm., a 7·5 cm., and a 40-pounder for this purpose in 1909. The 40-pounder was intended for fitting to ships or on fixed ground defences, the 6·5 cm. was produced on a field-gun type of carriage while the 7·5 cm. was intended for fitting to a lorry, ship, or ground battery. Basically similar to the 7·5-cm. field gun, the anti-balloon version had its trunnions moved back near to the breech to give the necessary elevation. The gun had a 'differential' recoil system without a buffer but with air run-out apparatus above the gun barrel. The run-out cylinder was kept under pressure and, when released, the gun ran out and fired automatically, the recoil recharging the run-out cylinder for the next shot. There was a telescopic sight on which drift and inclination could be set, but elevation was obtained from a separate rangefinder. The gun fired a 14·33 lb shell with a velocity of 2,130 f.p.s. to a range of 13,000 yards at 45° elevation. To show up the shell trajectory to the gunners, Krupp used a round which emitted smoke in flight, assisting the gunlayer to correct his aim-off between shots. In these early days shrapnel shells were used for anti-

balloon work. Krupp reasoned that high mobility was desirable for engaging fast-moving aircraft and airship targets, which dictated the fitting of the gun to a modified Daimler 50-h.p. lorry. Basically a standard commercial vehicle, ammunition lockers and crew seats were added at the rear, and the dropsides were arranged to act as a platform for the gun crew. This vehicle was used in the German Army Summer manoeuvres of 1909 and later it was armoured. A cylindrical barbette was added to the gun mount, an armoured shield was placed across the scuttle in front of the driver, and armoured ammunition lockers were fitted immediately behind the driving seat.

The Krupp-Daimler, with its purpose-built gun and fast top speed of 30 m.p.h., was the first really effective mobile anti-aircraft vehicle. The Germans used this sort of vehicle almost unchanged in the First World War, though later refinements included the provision of jacks to stabilise the vehicle when the gun fired. The 8·8-cm. gun which was to become the most famous German gun of the Second World War, was also used on a similar lorry mount in 1917–18 when it first appeared. The appearance of the Krupp-Daimler, which received a good deal of publicity at the time, undoubtedly influenced Major Davidson in the development of his Cadillac Balloon Destroyer in 1910. (Plate 15).

30 **Packard 24-h.p. 3-ton Truck with Driggs-Schroeder Gun,** 1909, U.S.A.

At the same time as Krupp was testing the balloon destroyer, two lorries with

3-pdr. quick-firing guns were being tested with the U.S. Army on their Summer manoeuvres at Massachusetts. The guns were Driggs-Schroeder 'pom-poms' mounted on the back of a Frayer-Miller and a Packard 3-tonner respectively, the latter being illustrated. Both vehicles were hired from the manufacturers who also provided the drivers. The guns were basically naval weapons, each weighing 500 lb and having a rate of fire of 100 rounds per minute, with a $3\frac{1}{2}$-mile range. They could be traversed on their mounts which were bolted to the body floor. During the manoeuvres, the vehicles gave a good account of themselves and operated over unmade roads and also across country where the going was firm enough to allow it. A platoon of infantry was allocated to each truck and they were used with much success during several stages of the exercise. They supported engineers engaged in demolition work, engaged enemy artillery—though outranged for this—and covered rearguard actions. However, the War Department considered that this type of vehicle was not a worthwhile substitute for artillery since the guns—the biggest that could be mounted—lacked the range of normal field artillery. The value of this type of equipment as a highly mobile hard-hitting weapon in its own right was not appreciated.

31 **Packard 24-h.p. 3-ton Truck,** 1909–18, U.S.A.

Though the idea of a truck-mounted gun was not proceeded with, the performance of the trucks themselves, particularly the Packard, impressed the U.S. Army. Hitherto transport had been almost entirely horse-drawn in the U.S. Army but the two gun-carrier trucks used in the manoeuvres were also pressed into service to carry troops and stores. This led to an order for a number of Packard 3-tonners, which were taken into service in the years 1910–12, and many more orders in subsequent years. The original vehicles were like the gun-carrier (Plate 30) but with dropside bodies. From 1911 mudguards were fitted but earlier vehicles lacked these. The Packard 3-tonner was a most successful type used widely commercially. It had a four-cylinder engine with the cylinders in pairs and speed was controlled by both a foot accelerator and a throttle lever on the steering column. Drive was via a carden shaft to a three-speed and reverse gearbox which shared a common housing with the differential. Final drive was by chains. Semi-elliptic springs were fitted and the wheels were wooden with solid tyres, dual at the rear. The wheelbase was 12 ft and the track was 68 ins. Speed was governed to 12 m.p.h. This basic design remained virtually unaltered until 1918 and hundreds of Packards served with the U.S. Army and other services during the Great War period. Among refinements introduced over the years were uprated engines, improved bodies, transmission brakes, and a change from left hand to right hand drive. In 1913 the front wheels were enlarged from 2 in. to 6 in. diameter, matching the rear wheels, and in 1914 worm drive was introduced. From 1915 all the controls and instruments were neatly grouped in a separate box ahead of the steering column. The illustration is of a Packard 3-tonner of 1916 with all the improvements mentioned, affording a direct contrast with the first Army Packard (Plate 30) to show how little the basic design altered during its long production life. The original design appeared in 1908, a year before the U.S. Army first became interested in it.

32 Ravaillier Amphibious Car, 1910, France

Many years ahead of its time came the Ravaillier amphibious car which was tested by the French Army Engineer Corps in 1910. With a wooden boat-shaped body and a propeller taken from the rear-mounted engine it presented a most unusual appearance. Tests took place at Versailles and in the River Rhône. Though the vehicle performed well, there was no military requirement for such a car—or 'canot-voiture-automobile' as it was called—and it was regarded by the military authorities more as an interesting and diverting toy than as a practical proposition. Top speed on land was 35 km.p.h. and on water it went at 9 km.p.h. Equipment included a tow rope, windlass, foghorn, and oars. The Ravaillier never saw service, but was one of the first practical amphibious vehicles.

33 NAG 4-ton Lorry, Military Subvention Type, 1909-12, Germany
and
34 NAG 4-ton Lorry with Gas Containers, 1909-12, Germany

The German War Department was among the first to introduce a war subsidy (or subvention) to finance a reserve of road vehicles which could be taken over quickly by the army if hostilities commenced. At first the requirements were casual and by 1907 some 158 assorted lorries had been registered for subsidies. In 1908 firm regulations were laid down for vehicles qualifying for subsidies. Maximum permitted weight was 4,000 kg. and the gross weight could not exceed 8,000 kg. Power was not to be less than 35 h.p. and a load of up to 4,000 kg. had to be possible. Drive could be by shaft or chain and rear wheels had to be twins. Each lorry had to be supplied with a trailer, and the dimensions of both had to be less than 2 metres wide with a track width of not more than 5 feet. These severe restrictions on width, which resulted in very narrow vehicles, were deliberately chosen to keep the vehicle to optimum width for use on French (rather than German) roads. The subsidy was £200 towards the vehicle cost and £50 per annum towards upkeep. £40,000 was reserved in the defence budget of 1908-9 specifically for subsidies. The first subvention trials under the scheme were held in the summer of 1909 over a varied 1,458-mile route and 12 firms entered lorries. Of these, the vehicle entered by NAG (Neue Automobil Gesellschaft) was the most powerful. Its motor developed up to 60-h.p., had Bosch ignition and forced lubrication, and a governor to prevent excessive strain on the ample power of the engine. The chassis was simple with parallel girder side frames. Eleven firms received approval to build subsidy types as a result of the trials, among them Daimler, Ehrhardt, and Bussing, as well as NAG. Large numbers of these types were built and all saw extensive service in the Great War. Plate 33 shows the standard NAG 4-tonner and 34 shows a specialised model produced in 1910 specifically to carry 80 gas cylinders (each 5 cubic feet capacity) for airships and observation balloons. The NAG and other types, as well as being sold to commercial firms were purchased direct by the army who also operated a limited scheme whereby army lorries could be hired out to civilian firms.

35 Napier Light Car, 1912, U.K.

Napier Light lorries had figured prominently in the London-Hastings military run of 1909 and in 1912 Ducros Ltd., who made Napiers at Acton, demonstrated an ingenious idea for a military car for 'universal' use. Based on the chassis of the then standard Napier light car model, the design consisted of a number of alternative bodies which enabled the chassis to be adapted swiftly for any of a number of alternative roles. The bodywork was on the Windham detachable principal with retractive supporting legs and runners allowing the body to be removed or replaced without the aid of jacks or cranes. This illustration shows the chassis fitted with a traversing mount for a searchlight. The same body could be used with a Maxim machine-gun on the same mount.

36 Napier Light Car, 1912, U.K.

Another alternative as shown was as a troop carrier. A further alternative was a tilt-covered van body intended as an ambulance or for light cargo. Though demonstrated to the Army this very clever idea was not adopted although Napier cars were in Army service.

Commercial ideas were still usually well ahead of military ideas at this time.

37 Hupmobile 20-h.p. Military Scout Car, 1912, U.S.A.

British, French and German Armies had used staff cars and trucks soon after the turn of the century. The U.S. Army, however, lagged behind in the adoption of motor transport, with just a few individuals like Majors Davidson and Gallagher demonstrating the value of motor transport largely on their own initiative. One of the first—if not *the* first—of the cars in official U.S. Army service was this 20-h.p. Hupmobile Runabout, a standard vehicle of its time purchased for military use in 1911. It was allocated to the 26th Infantry and used by one of the staff officers, Major Dickson, as a liaison and scouting vehicle. On the march the Hupmobile was used to lead the unit's motor truck column and clear the way ahead. On manoeuvres and camp exercises it was used to carry generals and other senior officers, and also to deliver rations, tow a trailer, carry photographers, and inspect and place firing targets. In a year it covered 3,500 miles almost entirely over rough roads and cross-country in usually adverse conditions. Though it was handled very toughly indeed the Hupmobile did not once break down nor did it show any sign of wear. Major Dickson was much impressed by this performance and personally wrote to the Hup Motor Co., Detroit, a letter on their vehicle's fine record. Later more cars of this type were acquired. The drawing shows Major Dickson at the wheel of this successful little vehicle.

38 Foden 5-ton Steam Wagon, 1912, U.K.

By 1912 the British had a subsidy scheme for lorries in operation, but there was still the need to borrow other vehicles for special occasions. The vehicle illustrated is a commercial Foden steam lorry hired from a South London haulage company for the duration of Summer manoeuvres. This particular vehicle was used by the 25th Cyclist Battalion, a London Territorial Army unit, to carry their bicycles and kit. Characteristic Foden features are shown with overtype horizontal boiler and solid rubber-tyred wheels. The army already possessed a few Fodens of this type but took over very many from civilian firms in late 1914 for the duration of the war.

39 Chatillon-Panhard Tractor, 1912–13, France

Prior to the First World War most artillery was still horse-drawn except for some heavy guns which were hauled by traction engines. It was a French artillery officer, Lt. Col. Deport, who was responsible for the first practical four-wheel drive motor tractor for guns. In 1910 Deport first approached the firm of Panhard et Levassor with the idea for such a vehicle. Deport himself worked for the ordnance firm of Chatillon-Commentry, having retired from the Army in 1894. At the time of the annual French military trials at Satory in 1911, Deport showed his prototype for a 'Chatillon-Panhard' four-wheel drive gun tractor to the official motor vehicle testing commission. It drove over the

Satory cross-country testing course with ease, taking slopes and small obstacles in its stride. At the end of March 1912, the artillery testing commission asked Deport to give tham a similar demonstration at Vincennes, this time towing guns. The trials took place in July 1912 and the tractor was put through its paces towing a 155-mm. field-gun and limber and also towing a big 220-mm. siege mortar plus its baseplate cradle and limber. The tractor also carried a 14-man crew; in the case of the 220-mm. mortar the total drawbar weight was over 12 tons. Over open rough ground the performance of the vehicle was excellent and it was decided to enter it in the 1913 Spring manoeuvres where it would be tested with two other gun tractors which the Army had been offered. One of these was a two-wheel drive vehicle and the other was a four-wheel drive Latil. These vehicles were thoroughly tested in the trials with one non-stop 100 km. run unloaded and a non-stop 60 km. run towing guns plus numerous cross-country and inter-city runs with and without guns. At the end of the period 8–30 March, the tractors were stripped and examined. All three vehicles proved satisfactory, but it was the Chatillon-Panhard which had put up the best performance and hauled the heaviest loads. The artillery commission were most enthusiastic. The French artillery had tried using a lorry to haul guns as early as 1907, but since only two-wheel drive vehicles had been available, movement was restricted to roads. Now here was a motor tractor which could pull heavy artillery over rough country. Fifty Chatillon-Panhards were ordered at once—and delivered the following August—and a provisional order was given for another 50. However, it was decided to hold further trials before confirming the second order. This time six different vehicles were tried. The previous years trials had been held in fine dry weather and it was felt that tests in really bad conditions were necessary to give a true idea of any vehicle's capabilities. In March 1914, the trials took place just as the thaw was setting in and heavy rain had turned the exercise ground into a quagmire. This time none of the tractors performed particularly well, usually because the guns they were towing got bogged down and brought progress to a halt. The wisdom of ordering so many tractors before all the problems of cross-country movement were overcome was therefore open to question and the second order for Chatillon-Panhards was cancelled. It was decided that more 'user' experience was necessary, and the first 50 vehicles were allocated to the 4th Heavy Artillery Regiment for extended service. This unit was equiped with 120-mm. guns and was the first artillery in the French Army to be fully mechanised. As such the regiment took pride of place in the Bastille Day parade in Paris on 14 July 1914. When War was declared on 4 August, these 50 Chatillon-Panhards were the largest single group of vehicles in French service. The French Army at that time had only 220 motor vehicles altogether, including 91 assorted lorries, 31 assorted ambulances, and the balance made up of 2 'auto-cannons' and a motley collection of staff cars and light service vehicles. The Chatillon-Panhard tractors were swiftly at war and gave good service.

The Chatillon-Panhard had a 40-h.p. motor (at 1000 r.p.m.) and a top speed of 17 km. per hour. Unloaded it could tow up to 15 tons but then its speed fell to 8 km. per hour. The turning circle had a radius of approximately only 16 ft.

40   Lefebvre Tractor, 1913, France

In July 1914 a tractor made its appearance which could have been the answer to the French artillery-testing commission's quest for a vehicle with good cross-country performance in any conditions. This vehicle also had the distinction of being the first with 'half-track' configuration, though it also had rear wheels. Mechanically it was based on Schneider tractor parts and its designer, Lefebvre, was inspired by the American Holt crawler tractor, two of which had been imported to Tunis for agricultural work in 1911. The Lefebvre tractor had steel wheels for normal running but carried crawler tracks at the rear which were arranged to run round small bogie wheels attached to a pivoted frame structure. The front end of the frame could be raised or lowered by worm gearing from handles adjacent to the driving position. On coming to rough or muddy going, the driver simply lowered the track frames —and hence the tracks. To give added traction, ballast weights could be carried in a box at the rear. Though intended for agricultural use only, it was suggested to the Army that the Lefebvre tractor be examined and evaluated for military use. This proposal coincided with the outbreak of war and in the rush to mobilise, nothing more was done about this very promising design, which thus faded into oblivion.

41 Daimler Motor Bus, Tramway (M.E.T.) Omnibus Co., 1914, U.K.

When war came in August 1914 all the armies involved still relied largely on horse-drawn transport. Progress had been made with a certain amount of mechanisation, but it was the subsequent fighting, spreading in extent and intensity on an unprecedented scale, which really gave impetus to the wider adoption of motor transport for military purposes. The British Army as recounted earlier had used buses in military exercises as early as 1908, (Plate 26), when a small number had been requisitioned to test the feasibility of the idea. In 1914, however, it was the Royal Navy which became the first to put this type of scheme into practice. The small British Expeditionary Force had partially held up the German advance into Belgium at the Battle of Mons on 22 August 1914, and soon afterwards when the threat to the Channel ports became apparent the Admiralty sent a force of Royal Marines and the Royal Naval Air Service to protect Boulogne, Ostend, Dunkirk, and the adjoining important areas. The limited number of vehicles at the Army's disposal (about 1,200 at this time) was already fully committed in support of the over-stretched B.E.F. Probably recalling the Army manoeuvres of 1908—he was a Territorial Army officer at the time—Mr Winston Churchill, the First Lord of the Admiralty, asked the London General Omnibus Co. to provide buses for the use of the naval forces he had sent to France. The L.G.O.C. readily agreed and called for volunteers from among their conductors and drivers to join up for the duration and take their buses

across the Channel. From the huge number of volunteers, 75 crews were chosen and were quickly recruited as Royal Marines. The L.G.O.C. put 75 buses at the Admiralty's disposal, selecting these from the Daimler fleet of the Tramways (M.E.T.) Omnibus Co. which was an associated company of the L.G.O.C. Early in September the buses and their crews were shipped to France and were rushed to the Franco-Belgian border where they carried out patrol work with Marines in the Lille, Tournai, and Ypres areas, and also acted as general transport vehicles. Antwerp was threatened and besieged and the M.E.T. Daimlers rushed Marines and French troops to the defence, their first actual taste of action. In these hectic early days there was little or no time to alter or even repaint the vehicles for military service, so they ran through France and Belgium still in the smart M.E.T. livery and complete with characteristic advertisements and London destination boards. Gradually such decorations were obliterated or defaced and the drawing shows a typical M.E.T. vehicle as it appeared in Antwerp in the first week of October 1914. When Antwerp fell on 9 October many of the M.E.T. Daimlers fell into German hands while the survivors were patched up, had their windows boarded up, were repainted in khaki, and were used by the Royal Naval Division in France for the remainder of the war.

42 L.G.O.C. B Type Motor Bus/Lorry, 1914–18, U.K.

The value and usefulness of the buses was proven in the Royal Marines'

Antwerp operations, and this led the Army to requisition buses for their own use. On 18 October 1914, the L.G.O.C. allocated 300 of their A.E.C. B Type buses to the Army while 150 more volunteer crews joined up, this time enlisted in the Army Service Corps. From Grove Park depot, London, 150 of the buses were sent to the docks with their volunteer crews the day after the call-up for the journey to France. The other 150 B Type buses had their bodies removed and stored and were converted into lorries, vans, or other special purpose types for army service. The drawing shows one of these 'lorries' after alterations, with the L.G.O.C. bus origin apparent from the bonnet. The first 300 vehicles requisitioned were followed by hundreds more in the months that followed. Over 1,300 B Types eventually saw military service in the years 1914–18 which was nearly half the L.G.O.C.'s total fleet of this sort of bus. Paradoxically, the B Type bus which served in such vast numbers as a perpetual reminder to a largely citizen army of the link with home, remains one of the best known military vehicles of all time. One of these vehicles, nicknamed 'Old Bill' after Bairnsfather's famous World War I cartoon character, has been preserved by the Auxiliary Omnibus Companies Association and is to be seen at the Imperial War Museum, London, as a reminder of the important part played by London buses in this war. The B Types, organised in 'Auxiliary Omnibus Companies' of 75 vehicles each served all over the Western Front as troop and supply carriers until the Armistice in 1918. Then after overhaul, many of them went back into normal service on the London streets. A.E.C., the B Types' builders, actually made some new vehicles as lorries like the one illustrated using spare parts from stock. The B Type taught a useful lesson for the future—the value of a standardised chassis, which greatly simplifies maintenance when large numbers of vehicles are needed. The bus companies had learned this long before the Army found the need for themselves.

43 L.G.O.C. B Type Motor Bus, 1914–18, U.K.

The first batches of A.E.C. B Type buses sent to France arrived in their famous red and white livery complete with advertisements and London destination boards. Like the M.E.T. Daimlers before them, they presented an incongruous sight in the forward areas. Soon, however, they were modified with the lower deck windows removed —they were too easily broken—and boarded up. Toolboxes and stowage racks were added in convenient positions and an overall coat of khaki paint was applied. Later vehicles were sent out from England already modified. When the stock of buses had been built up some were diverted for special purposes such as ambulances and staff caravans. One duty for which a bus was well suited was as a mobile pigeon loft, some of which worked with every divisional H.Q. This was before the days of efficient portable wireless signalling sets and pigeons were still a major means of communication. As a pigeon loft the top of the bus was roofed in and cages were built on each side from wood and chicken wire. An entrance was built at the front while the lower deck was fitted as a store and office.

44 Boulant Mobile Surgery, 1912–18, France

Motor ambulances had been in service for some years by 1912, but an innovation at that time was a complete fully-equipped mobile surgery which the French Army Medical Service (Service de Santé) tried out. It was built for them by Schneider on the same Boulant chassis as used for the Paris buses. It had a 40-h.p. engine, a top speed of 30 km. per hour, solid rubber tyres and twin rear wheels. Full-width double doors were fitted at the back of the body with wide steps to make entry easy for stretcher bearers. The body was divided into three compartments. At the back the entrance lobby contained a 200-litre water tank, wash basins and linen and medical cabinets. The centre section formed an operating theatre about 12 ft long and $7\frac{1}{2}$ ft wide, complete with operating table and electric light. The front compartment, with access doors each side, held the sterilisers. Folded tenting was fixed to each side of the body and this could be erected when the vehicle was stationary to form reception bays for patients with minor injuries or those awaiting attention. While this vehicle was admirable in every way, and well ahead of its time, it was also very expensive and no further vehicles of this type were built at the time. However, it appears that a number of similar vehicles were produced during the Great War, probably as direct conversions from Paris buses. Pictures show them giving valuable service on the Western Front in 1915–16.

45 Leyland 3-ton subsidy A Van, 1914–18, U.K.

The British subsidy scheme is described in detail later. By the outbreak of war in August 1914 many firms were operating vehicles built to the War Office subsidy requirements. One such was the big London store of Warings whose vans were all Leylands. When war was declared, their transport department was formed into a complete Army Service Corps company and the Warings vans all set off for Avonmouth Docks for shipment to France where they were among the first British transport vehicles to arrive. For some weeks they operated in France still in their civilian livery with only 'Army Service Corps' stickers to provide identity of the new ownership. The drawing shows one of Warings' Leyland vans at this period of 1914.

46 Foster-Daimler 105-h.p. Petrol Tractor, 1914–18, U.K.

The firm of Foster & Co. of Lincoln was prominent in the engineering field and prior to the First World War enjoyed much success in export fields with agricultural and commercial tractors. Sir William Tritton, its very able and inventive Managing Director, had been one of the observers at the 1909 military tractor trials (Plates 24 and 25) and in 1912 his firm produced a petrol tractor similar to the winning Thornycroft design but very much bigger and with an engine twice as powerful. It had a 105-h.p. Daimler engine, sprung traction-engine type wheels (the rear pair 8 ft in diameter) and a sturdy channel plate chassis. Prior to the outbreak of war several of these had been sold abroad, notably in South America. Soon after war was declared Admiral Sir Reginald Bacon, head of the Coventry Ordnance Works, approached Winston Churchill, First Lord of the Admiralty, with the idea of using large 15-inch howitzers in France for heavy bombardment and siege work (Bacon's firm normally made 15-inch naval guns). Churchill was attracted by the idea and ordered ten of these guns. Bacon earmarked the Foster-Daimler as the most suitable towing vehicle, for though the 15-inch howitzers broke into components for transportation, their bulk and weight remained considerable. Eight tractors were needed for each gun when the ammunition trailers were included. In the event, the first 15-inch howitzers were ready early in 1915 and Fosters built the tractors to haul them. The howitzers themselves were towed in parts—barrel, cradle, carriage, and so on, and assembled on the site. The Royal Marines Artillery manned and operated these heavy weapons. Like the old traction engines, the Foster-Daimler tractor could be fitted with flanged wheels for operating on standard-gauge railway track.

Though a highly specialised type the Foster-Daimler was historically important, for its appearance had a direct bearing on other crucial developments in the history of mechanised warfare. First of all, its great size inspired Churchill with his first idea for a 'trench-crossing machine'—which later crystallised in the tank. Second it introduced Sir William Tritton to Churchill and his 'Landships Committee', as a result of which Tritton played a major part in early tank design. Third, its well proven Daimler engine powered all the early

tanks as it was available in quantity. In 1915, at Churchill's instigation one Foster-Daimler tractor was converted as a true 'trench-crosser', with a single narrow front wheel and moving chain-operated ramps for the rear wheels. Though ingenious and well thought out, the vehicle proved very poor and impractical on tests, and development was abandoned.

47 Holt 75-h.p. Petrol Tractor, 1914–18, U.S.A./U.K./France

With the big expansion of the British Army in late 1914 and early 1915, there was a severe shortage of tractors suitable for hauling the heavier artillery pieces. It was soon found that horses were inadequate in the congested and usually muddy conditions of the Western Front for pulling medium or heavy guns due to the large teams required. The animals remained with the horse and field artillery batteries for the duration, therefore, while tractors were used for larger weapons. Steam traction engines were pressed into service initially but the first 'standard' tractor adopted in quantity was the Holt, an American-built agricultural tractor with petrol engine and crawler tracks. A few of these had been imported to Europe as early as 1912 for commercial use, and the Holt company had appointed agencies in various countries. Soon after war was declared, the Royal Artillery in casting round for suitable readily available tractors selected the Holt 75-h.p. model and orders were placed. The fact that this vehicle had tracks, and therefore a limited off-the-road capability was a less important consideration than its availability. In January 1915 the first deliveries were made and after assessment trials at Aldershot the Holts were sent to France where they became a major artillery vehicle for the next four years, mainly engaged in hauling medium guns like the 6-inch howitzer, the 60-pdr., the 8-inch, and the 9·2-inch. To the men these vehicles were popularly known as 'Cats' (Caterpillar Tractors). The Holt 75-h.p. tractor weighed about 15 tons and it had a top speed of just under 2 m.p.h. for towing and 5 m.p.h. unladen. Steering was effected by one clutch lever per track which disconnected the drive to the inside of the desired turn while the outer track continued to drive. For sharper turns a wood 'skotch' was usually thrown under the idle track. The front jockey wheel aided stability and was used in large radius turns; for sharp turns it still had to be used, however, to avoid wheel damage. By later standards the Holt had a poor cross-country ability, but its appearance was one of the factors which led indirectly to the development of the tank. Colonel E. D. Swinton, while serving temporarily in France, heard that the Holt had been adopted by the Royal Artillery and conceived the notion of an armoured version of the vehicle as an 'armoured machine-gun carrier' which would carry troops and their guns to storm trenches. At that period, late 1914, the fighting on the Western Front had already degenerated into the trench warfare conditions which led directly to the appearance of tanks as a means to overcome the power of the all-dominant machine-gun. In the event, tank development in Britain took another course (though Holts were tested—and rejected —for possible cross-country use with armoured troop carrying trailers). However, the Holt tractor remains historically one of the most important military vehicles of all time. One Holt 75-h.p. vehicle was purchased and tested (in Tunisia) by the French Army for possible adoption as an artillery tractor. But France later produced vehicles inspired by the Holt and did not herself use this type in quantity. Two armoured versions of the Holt were produced in America for possible use as tanks (though they were not adopted), and Holt components formed the basis of the only German tank to see service, the A7V and provided the inspiration for the French tanks which appeared in 1916. In British use, however, the Holts remained in service only as artillery tractors, some lasting well into the twenties. By 1918 they were being used also, to haul 3-inch A.A. guns. In Mesopotamia they were used with tracked trailers to take supplies over the desert in addition to their artillery duties.

48 Renault Ambulance, 1914–18, France

Like the British, the French, as already recounted, were severely short of motor transport at the outbreak of war. The answer to the problem was requisitioning on a grand scale and in the closing months of 1914 a total of 1,049 buses, 2,500 cars, and 6,000 lorries were acquired from commercial sources. On 9 September 1914, motor cars made military history when all the taxis in Paris were commandeered to rush the French 62nd Division to the Marne to stem the German threat to encircle Paris. The vehicle illustrated was one of many Renault Paris taxis subsequently adapted for other purposes. In this particular instance the saloon bodywork was removed and a simple framework body replaced it, arranged to hold stretchers. A canvas tilt completed the conversion, and large numbers of these makeshift ambulances were used by the French Army in the early days of the war. A similar conversion was used to provide a mobile generating plant or wireless car. The same sort of framework body was installed, complete with canvas tilt, and externally these vehicles looked similar to the ambulance though they carried a generator and batteries and wireless respectively instead of stretchers. Later Renault produced similar vehicles to these as new, basing them on the same taxi chassis.

49 Renault Searchlight Carrier, 1914–18, France

The Napier searchlight carrier illustrated in Plate 35 had been inspired by three similar vehicles on Panhard 18-h.p. car chassis which had been produced for the French Army in 1911. In those days the value of the searchlight was stressed more on coast defence than on air defence, for which it subsequently became mostly used. By 1914 searchlights had became a useful battlefield accessory for night illumination or long range signalling. The Renault firm built a number of searchlight carriers specially designed on their 2-ton commercial chassis, while others were adapted from taxi chassis like the ambulance in Plate 48. All carried the standard searchlight, made by Harlé of Paris and mounted on a light four-wheel carriage. It could be used as it was, mounted on the vehicle, or it could be unloaded and emplaced for ground deployment. The vehicle carried a generator and extra batteries in the compartment behind the driver and there was a reel with 300 metres of wire cable which meant that the light could be concealed up to 300 yards from the vehicle which could itself be hidden. The light could be controlled, as far as illumination was concerned, from the vehicle, by means of a control switch and wire, or it could be controlled from any other position within 300 yards as the control box was detachable. On the vehicle the searchlight carriage was held steady in grooved channels and for unloading two channel plates were fitted to the rear. These were normally carried on the rear platform under the searchlight carriage. The vehicle had a crew of five, the searchlight had a 35-inch reflector, and the electrical system for it was 80 volts. The British Army used very similar vehicles to this, but most of the British searchlights were carried in Austin 3-ton trucks which also carried the battery/generator/control box behind the driving cab.

50 Jeffery Tractor, 1915–18, U.S.A./France/U.K.

The French Army was largely dependent on horses for hauling its field artillery. The muddy conditions of the Western Front limited the mobility even of the famous 75-mm. gun which was notable for its lightness and handiness. Early in 1915 it was decided to study ways of motorising the 75-mm. batteries partly to utilise existing guns in the best possible way by making them available for more rapid deployment, and partly to overcome the shortage of horses which was foreseen in any case if the war dragged on. In June 1915 the plan was put into practice when a battery of the

13th Artillery Regiment was fully motorised with ten Jeffery-Quad tractors
to carry the guns and seven 3-ton lorries
to carry the crews and ammunition.
The guns were carried on the rear platform of the tractor being loaded and off-
loaded by means of ramps which were
carried on the platform also. To accommodate the barrel, a cut-out was made
in the back of the cab. The thinking
behind this *portée* idea (which was later
used more extensively in World War
2) was to eliminate the limber and the
need to tow the gun. This was a lesson
learned from the earlier trials with the
Chatillon-Panhard tractor (Plate 39)
where the tractor had performed well in
muddy conditions but the gun and
limber had stuck. In September and
October 1915 two more batteries were
formed, and a second complete *portée*
regiment was formed in June 1916 and
another in April 1917. In August 1917
it was decided to convert all 75-mm.
gun regiments in Army Corps to
portée units. Seven new *portée* regiments
were ready by the end of 1917 and
there were no less than twenty at the
time of the German spring offensive in
March 1918. By June 1918 there were
27 *portée* regiments and by the time of
the Armistice 33 had been formed. This
formidable artillery force was transported by 8,600 vehicles (tractors
lorries, and staff cars) with just under
44,000 personnel. *Portée* artillery of this
kind was considered most useful by the
French General Staff as it had a mobility
and range far superior than anything
possible with horses. The major limita-
tion on deploying *portée* artillery at that
time was, in fact, the speed and relia-
bility of the tractors, which were poor
by modern standards.

Illustrated is the Jeffery-Quad tractor
which was built in America by the
Thomas B. Jeffery Co. and became one
of the most widely used military vehicles
of the war. The Americans, British, and
French all used this successful four-
wheel drive type. In Britain and America
the Jeffery-Quad was also used as an
artillery tractor but normally as a
towing, rather than a *portée,* vehicle.
Some Jeffery-Quads were also used to
form the basis of armoured cars. A
similar type of tractor also used by both
the French *portée* regiments and the
British Royal Artillery was the Nash,
another American four-wheel drive
vehicle of similar size.

51 Schneider PB2 Omnibus, 1914–
18, France

The Paris buses commandeered for the
French Army were put to many uses.
Some were used as troop transports,
others as ambulances, and some as
mobile workshops. A number were put
to novel use as livestock carriers; these
transported sheep to the front line for
slaughter to keep the men in the trenches
supplied with fresh meat. Like the
British the French also converted some
buses as mobile pigeon lofts. These had
a second deck built on them, complete
with cages. The drawing shows one of
the buses, its windows boarded up,
which were used as livestock carriers.

52 Wolseley 3-ton Lorry, 1913–18,
U.K.

It was appreciated in the early 1900s,
when motor transport first became a
practical military proposition, that any
large-scale war in the future would
necessitate the massive acquisition of

extra vehicles at short notice. Peacetime financial stringency did not permit large sums to be spent on expensive transport fleets for which there was little employment in normal times. A subvention (or subsidy) scheme was the answer. In this, owners of vehicles meeting military requirements received an annual subsidy for a given period from the military authorities in return for which they maintained the vehicles in good working order and surrendered them to the Government for a fixed sum in the time of national emergency. In 1908 the British War office started a subvention scheme for traction engines and in 1911 announced a scheme for motor vehicles. In this an initial subsidy of £8–£12 (according to drive) would be paid for each lorry registered with a £15 annual subsidy thereafter. This was parsimonious compared with the similar scheme operated in Germany where the initial payment was £200 with a £50 annual subsidy. Subsequently, therefore, by 1914 the British subsidy was raised to £110, comprising £30 initial payment and the balance of the total over three years. To qualify for a subsidy the vehicles had to meet rigid specifications laid down by the War Office. The result had a major effect on vehicle design generally, raising the standard considerably, not only in Britain but in France, Austria, and Germany as well where similar subvention schemes were operated.

The British War Office subsidy scheme divided vehicles into two classes: Class A to carry 3 tons and Class B to carry 30 cwt. The actual regulations were complex but salient points in the scheme specified a four-cylinder petrol engine, with cylinders cast in pairs,

engine-control connections by rods instead of wire, governed engine, waterproofed high-tension magneto ignition, interchangeable radiator, four-speed gearbox, plus reverse, with standardised positions for foot and driving controls, standardised wheel and tyre sizes, standard type of lighting, canvas weatherprotection for the crew, compulsory provision of towing hooks front and rear, and interchangeable body. Dimension limits were specified and regulations were complete down to details of washer and screw sizes. The most important requirement of all, however, concerned the transmission which had to be by live axle via bevel drive. Chain drive was not acceptable.

A high degree of standardisation resulted from the specifications and from July 1912 only lorries which met the requirements qualified for the subsidy. This had the intended effect of whittling down the number of makes of lorry involved and made maintenance easier by reducing the number of spare parts needed for servicing. The vehicles being offered for subsidy had to undergo exhaustive acceptance trials which took place in January 1913 and April/May 1914. By the time war was declared in August 1914, several vehicle manufacturers had had their designs accepted for subsidy, these being Dennis, Maudslay, Hallford, Karrier, Leyland, Thornycroft and Wolseley. At once a total of 1,200 lorries of these types were acquired by the Army and the vehicle manufacturers carried on building directly for military requirements. Later other manufacturers joined the war effort building vehicles to War Office subsidy scheme standards.

The Subsidy Class A Wolseley shown

was first announced at the 1913 Commercial Vehicle Show at Olympia and thus one of the first types built to meet the War Office requirements. It had a four-cylinder engine governed to 1000 r.p.m. and fitted with Bosch watertight ignition. A Wolseley patent 'constant depression carburetter was fitted intended to maintain fuel mixture quality at all speeds. The clutch was of the leather-faced cone type and transmission was via a double reduction level drive live axle. In accordance with the subsidy requirements the rear axle could be removed by taking off the hub caps and without removing the rear wheels or jacking up the chassis. The differential could be similarly removed. This Wolseley 3-tonner marked this firm's return to lorry building for a short period and many hundreds of these vehicles were used by the British on the Western Front. Chassis plans of typical Subsidy A vehicles can be seen in Plates 54b and 55a.

53 Vickers-Clyno Machine Gun Combination, 1915–18, U.K.

The importance of the machine-gun had been greatly under-rated by the British and when war was declared in 1914, British infantry battalions were equipped with only two Maxim machine-guns each. The machine-gun, in German hands, soon became a dominant weapon and was largely responsible for the static trench warfare conditions into which the opposing sides had been forced by the end of 1914, the trenches offering the most adequate cover against the raking fire of this type of gun. Attacks on enemy trenches led to huge losses as infantrymen were pitted against the defensive power of the machine-

gun and it was these conditions which gave direct impetus to the development of the armoured car and tank.

The British Army greatly increased its stocks of machine-guns and the great importance of this weapon was recognised with the formation of the Machine Gun Corps on 22 October 1915. The M.G.C. was divided up into three branches, two to support the infantry and cavalry, and a third more independent arm, the Motor Machine Gun Corps, which was mainly used to support the infantry under Army command. To equip the new arm it had been decided to use motor cycle combinations and trials had been held soon after the outbreak of war to decide the best motor cycle and sidecar for service use. These were won by the firm of Clyno who produced a 5/6-h.p. machine with three-speeds and final drive in an enclosed casing. The sidecar had three-point spring suspension and all the wheels were interchangeable. With spring forks, telescopic stand, and easily removable V-twin engine, the Clyno was a very advanced machine for its time. On formation the Motor Machine Gun Corps was equipped with four batteries of Clynos and hundreds more were subsequently built. For military service, the Clyno carried a spare wheel on the offside alongside the pillion and the Vickers machine-gun with an armoured shield was fitted to the frame chassis of the sidecar by means of the standard tripod mount. Normally the gun faced forward but it could be mounted facing to the rear as shown in the illustration. It could also be dismounted from the sidecar and used in the normal ground firing role. A low seat for the gunner was fitted to the sidecar floor and behind the seat was stowage for ammunition, water (for the gun-cooling system), gun spares, and spare petrol, oil, and carbide, the latter for the headlights.

A complete gun detachment was equipped with three Clyno combinations. One carried the gun (as illustrated), the second was an identical combination but without the gun and acted as spare vehicle, while the third lacked an armour shield on the front of the sidecar and carried ammunition only. Clynos with normal passenger type sidecars and solo Clynos were also widely used in other arms of the British Army in the 1914–18 period for liaison and despatch carrier work.

The Vickers-Clyno Machine-Gun Combination represented an interesting vindication of the ideas for mobile machine-gun carriers postulated by individuals like Davidson, Genty, Northover and others during the pre-war period when official authorities were little interested in such projects. Appropriately enough it was the Machine Gun Corps which later manned the first British tanks in 1916 and from which the Tank Corps later grew.

54a Dennis 3-ton Lorry and **54b Dennis 3-ton Chassis,** 1913–18, U.K.

One of the best-known and most successful lorries built to meet Class A (3 tons) of the War Office subsidy scheme was the Dennis, which introduced several advanced features. Over 7,000 were built and the prototype was first exhibited at the 1913 Commercial Vehicle Show at Olympia. It conformed to all the subsidy requirements in its specification and included water-cooling for the transmission brake and forced lubrication for the engine. The four-

cylinder engine gave 55 h.p. at 1,360 r.p.m. and the performance of the Dennis was one of the best of all subsidy types. Loaded it could climb gradients sometimes as steep as 1 in 6. The Dennis 3-tonner was in production until the war's end. The features of the chassis designed to subsidy requirements can clearly be seen.

55a Thornycroft 3-ton Lorry, J Type chassis
and

55b Thornycroft 3-ton J Type Lorry with AA Gun, 1913–18, U.K.

The firm of John Thornycroft Ltd. of Basingstoke had a long history of producing vehicles to meet military requirements (see Plates 11 and 24) and it was not inappropriate that Thornycroft's J Type lorry should come out best in the 1913 and 1914 War Office subsidy trials. Not only did it lead the field in most of the trials runs, but it was also the lightest vehicle competing in the 3-ton Class A. The prototype vehicle was designed in 1912 specifically to qualify for the newly announced subsidy scheme. It took part in the 1913 trials and was exhibited at the Commercial Motor Show, Olympia, the following July. The wheelbase of the J Type was 13 ft 7½ in., and the width was 7 ft 2½ in. The four-cylinder side-valve engine developed 40 h.p. In all respects the vehicle conformed to the War Office subsidy requirements; it weighed 3¼ tons less in body, and had a top speed of 14½ m.p.h. More than 5,000 J Types were supplied to the British Army in the years 1914–18 and this vehicle won a great reputation on all fronts. The Thornycrofts were chosen for the more exacting special-purpose roles and those most associated with the J Type were the mobile workshops and the mobile anti-aircraft guns. The vehicle illustrated shows the latter configuration with 3-inch A.A. gun, one of the best-known vehicle types of the First World War. The mobile A.A. gun reflected the rapid growth of military airpower during the war years. The Germans had designed this sort of vehicle many years earlier (Plate 28) but in the British Army the mobile A.A. gun was very much a last-minute improvisation produced in 1915. The gun was a 13-pdr. field gun, as used by the Royal Horse Artillery, removed from its normal field carriage and fitted to a rotating pedestal mount. It was used in conjunction with a visual rangefinder carried in an accompanying vehicle and set up in a convenient position alongside the emplaced gun carrier. Jacks on the chassis steadied the vehicle when the gun was fired. The usual gun section was equipped with two Thornycroft gun-carrier lorries, each supported by two 3-ton lorries which carried the gun crew, the rangefinder, and ammunition. The Thornycroft mobile workshop was another very important type and had a van-like body with drop sides which opened out to form a working platform. Inside the body a lathe, anvil, work bench, drilling machine, grinding machine, and small auxiliary petrol engine driving a generator were the usual fittings, though equipment was changed for special functions on some vehicles. The mobile workshop companies carried out all minor running repairs (and not a few major repairs) to vehicles and guns behind the front lines. Thornycrofts served on all fronts with the British Army, and the J Type remained in production as a commercial vehicle until 1926. Early J Types had wheels with cast spokes, but these were soon changed for pressed-steel disc types as shown in the drawing.

56 **Vauxhall D Type Staff Car,** 1915–18, U.K.

As well as lorries, numerous cars were requisitioned for staff and liaison work. The British Army subsequently adopted the Vauxhall D Type, a 25-h.p. vehicle, as a standard type (among others) and this was produced mostly with an open touring body. Some were produced with enclosed saloon bodywork, however, as shown in the drawing and these were used exclusively by generals.

57 **Leyland Subsidy A Type,** 1915–18, U.K.
and
58 **Leyland Mobile Workshop,** 1915–18, U.K.

The other major manufacturer of War Office subsidy vehicles was Leyland, one of whose pre-1914 vehicles has already been shown (Plate 45). During the war vast numbers of Leylands (over 12,000) were turned out to the standard design and many of these were used by the Royal Flying Corps and its successor the Royal Air Force. In fact they became so well associated with the air force that the vehicle became popularly known as the Leyland 'RAF Type'. The Army did also use this type, however. The illustrations show two widely used variants, the ordinary 3-ton truck in R.F.C. service, and a workshop truck which was equipped exactly as described above for the very similar Thornycroft J Type Workshop Lorry. After the Armistice Leylands brought back many of the redundant vehicles from service use and remanufactured them for sale commercially. Some remained in use 20 years later. The Leyland followed the War office subsidy specification very closely. It had a 32- or 36-h.p. engine and a water-cooled transmission brake.

59 **Renault Porteur Tractor,** 1916–18, France

At the time the British adopted the Holt 75-h.p. Caterpillar Tractor (Plate 47), the French were also seeking a suitable tractor for hauling artillery. The chief engineer of Schneider, the big French arms and engineering firm, went to Britain in January 1915 to watch a demonstration of this vehicle at Aldershot. While there he met the representative of the Holt firm who showed him plans of the Baby Holt, a 45-h.p. smaller version of the 75-h.p. vehicle. As a result Schneider purchased one each of the 75-h.p. and 45-h.p. machines on behalf of the French Government. These arrived in May 1915 for tests. Meanwhile a French reserve artillery officer had requisitioned a couple of Holt tractors on his own initiative in Tunisia and had these shipped to France where they were used early in 1915 by his regiment in the Vosges, hauling 155-mm. guns. This officer sent a report to the Chief of Staff of the Army in August 1915 and suggested that the Baby Holt should be adopted forthwith for general artillery use. As a result of these activities an order for 15 vehicles was placed with Holt and the first two arrived in France in February 1916. One

of these was sent straight to Schneider who were working on the design of a tank for the French Army for which it was planned to copy the Holt-type suspension and tracks. However, as an artillery tractor the Holt was not considered to be the complete answer for French requirements. It was essentially intended for agricultural use. By this time the French Artillery had placed much faith in *portée* artillery (Plate 59) and requested a version of a crawler track tractor suited to the *portée* role. Schneider produced a flat platform tractor with front driving position based on the same chassis as the Schneider tank which they had meanwhile completed. However, this firm had now received an order for 400 of the tanks and thus had no spare productive capacity for building tractors. By this time Renault had also produced a *portée* tractor for Army requirements. It was now the Summer of 1916 and the success of the 75 mm. *portée* led the artillery to consider this means of transport for 155-mm. guns. Thus 50 Renault Porteur tractors were ordered almost instantly on 22 September 1916, and a month later the chief of artillery asked for a further 350 vehicles, plus 500 Schneiders. It was planned to carry 155-mm. guns on the Renaults (as illustrated) and 75-mm. guns on the slightly smaller Schneiders. The first 50 Renaults were to be used to carry the 155-mm. guns of two divisions, organised in batteries of eight. Meanwhile General Joffre had become C-in-C and reviewed the armaments situation. In January 1917 he pointed out that the Schneider tanks were more urgently needed than the tractors so the latter were reduced to a low priority commitment. The first Renault Porteurs were delivered in March 1917, and 120 had been delivered by the end of 1917. By the end of the war in November 1918, a total of 256 had been delivered out of the 350 ordered. Meanwhile the first Schneider Porteur had been completed in April 1917 and 110 of these were finally delivered by the war's end. The Renault tractor proved to be a most useful vehicle, carrying out many tasks with ease in the muddy conditions of the Western Front in addition to its prime task of carrying guns. Ammunition and store carrying was a common task. The Renault weighed 14 tons and could carry loads of up to 8 tons. It had a front-mounted 110-h.p. standard Renault engine which drove the front sprockets. It could also be used to drive a small capstan situated on the centre line just behind the engine, this being used to assist in loading the gun. The driver sat alongside the engine to the right, in a completely exposed position, while the rest of the vehicle consisted of a flat platform body. Wooden ramps were used to load the guns and a trestle kept the trail clear of the engine. The vehicle had four gears and top speed was just under 6 km. per hour. Tracks and suspension were of the Holt type. The slightly smaller Schneider Porteur weighed 10 tons and could carry 3 tons with a top speed of 8 km. per hour. In addition to the 75-mm. gun it could carry later model 155-mm. guns which had retracting barrels for transportation.

60 Stoewer Staff Car, 1916–18, Germany

Though the German Army had a subsidy scheme operating prior to the start of the war, during the war itself they supplemented the subsidy types with numerous other vehicles which were simply commercial types purchased for military service. This Stoewer tourer was typical of the latter class of vehicle and was used as a staff car. It illustrates a characteristic common to most German vehicles in the latter half of the war, namely all-steel sprung wheels. The blockade of Germany by the Allies led to a major shortage of vital materials like steel for tanks and ships and rubber needed for tyres. To overcome the rubber shortage several types of resilient steel wheel were developed. In the example shown leaf springs are featured, but coil springs were also used.

61 Latil Tractor, 1916–18, France/ U.S.A.

The wide employment of tracked crawler tractors by the French artillery brought its own problems. Of necessity slow, they also had limited mileage due to track and suspension breakages when making long runs. To conserve their tracks as much as possible and speed their deployment to the fighting zone, it was decided late in 1917 to make suitable trailers able to carry 8 tons for Baby Holt and Schneider tractors and up to 14 tons for Renault tractors. The firm of Buire built the trailers and suitable heavy towing vehicles were sought. Two main types were chosen. One was the Knox which was a prime mover originally used to tow parts of heavy guns, and the other was the Latil 7-ton artillery tractor, a four-wheel drive vehicle originally produced for towing 155-mm. guns. Together with a very similar type of tractor built by

Renault, the Latil was developed in 1914–1915. There were never sufficient trailers to go around, however, and by March 1918 only 66 had been built. Though used with effect to carry up tractors (and, occasionally, tanks) on at least two occasions in 1918, the plan to provide trailers had not been realised by the war's end. The Latil tractor is shown here, but not the trailer.

62 Fiat 18BL Lorry, 1916–18, Italy

Unlike the British, French and Germans the Italian Army had no subsidy scheme operation when the First World War started. In 1914 the Italian Army was very short of vehicles and the War Department asked Fiat to give top priority to developing a standard military wagon comparable to foreign war subsidy types. The resulting 18BL was a rugged and sturdy design with a 5,655 c.c. four-cylinder engine which developed 38 h.p. at 1,300 r.p.m. It had four speeds and reverse but final drive was by chains in enclosed casings. Produced in hundreds from 1915–21, the Fiat 18BL was used by the British and French in Italy as well as by the Italian Army. Top speed was 24 km. per hour. An improved model was also built, the Fiat 18BLR, which had smaller wheels, a longer body, and heavier springs. It was mechanically identical to the 18BL but slightly slower with a top speed of 21 km. per hour.

63 Fiat 18BL Generator Lorry, 1916–18, Italy and
64 Mobile Searchlight, 1916–18, Italy

This drawing illustrates one of several special vehicles based on the Fiat 18BL.

This vehicle was used on the Italian Front in 1917, towing and powering a heavy searchlight. An old generator engine is mounted in the back of the vehicle and a second compartment is built behind the driving cab to accommodate the detachment. Electric leads were carried to power the light when set up for use. The searchlight itself was carried on an old converted horse cart.

65 Latil Artillery Tractor, 1916–18, France/U.S.A.

Circumstances leading to the adoption of 75-mm. *portée* guns have previously been given (Text to Plate 50). The American-built Jeffery-Quad used as standard equipment was not considered fully satisfactory and efforts were made to find an indigenous design to replace it. The Latil tractor, a four-wheel drive design, appeared in 1915 (Plate 61), and a version was modified with smaller wheels and platform body for the *portée* role. In this form the ramps used for loading the gun on the vehicle were carried on the platform edges. With the 1917–18 expansion of the *portée* artillery regiments the Latil tractor was widely used to supplement and replace the Jeffery.

66 Latil Artillery Tractor with Delahaye Tracks, 1918, France

The appearance of the Holt tractors in British and French military service in 1915 prompted several motor manufacturers to consider ways of fitting tracks to existing road vehicles, thus giving an off-road capability without the huge development costs needed for purpose-built tractors. Delahaye produced a particularly ingenious track unit designed to fit the driving-axle of a road vehicle and with gearing from the axle shaft to the rear sprocket in the track unit. Thus the track unit took the place of the wheel and no change was needed to the normal transmission. The framework of the track unit held the centre gear wheel, the sprocket, idler, and three small support rollers. Each track unit weighed 500 kg. complete and was fully self-contained. The first need was for artillery tractors with cross-country performance, so the first type of vehicle to be fitted with Delahaye tracks for trials was a Latil tractor, a new four-wheel drive vehicle which had just been developed (Plate 66). A Delahaye track unit was fitted in place of each of the four driven wheels on one of the first of these vehicles to be built. Trials were conducted in November 1915 and the vehicle was able to tow loads of 20 tons or more over gentle slopes. However, steering was extremely difficult and the axles were not strong enough for the stresses imposed on the vehicle across country. To aid traction 2 tons of ballast were fitted, but this did not solve the problem. The modified vehicle was not adopted as such, therefore, but Delahaye carried out experiments with a view to improving the tracks and steering. The major change was to rubber track shoes instead of the steel shoes originally fitted. In January 1918, by which time tanks had become a major weapon of war, the Armaments Ministry ordered six Latils fitted with the modified Delahaye tracks. Trials showed that loads of up to 23 tons could be hauled. With the modified tracks the vehicles had a better performance though they were still not very good across

country. Three were issued to each of two heavy artillery divisions where they were mainly used as ammunition carriers. In the meantime Delahaye had experimented in fitting a pair of their tracks to the rear axle of a rear-wheel drive Saurer $3\frac{1}{2}$-ton truck, making in effect a half-track. Trials in November and December 1917 showed this vehicle, retaining its front wheels, to be much easier to handle than the Latil. It performed quite well cross-country but the rear springs were inadequate over rough going. It was recommended by the testing commission that pairs of tracks should be provided for the Saurer, but these were to be used only when the conditions justified the trouble of fitting them—a task which took about an hour. In May 1918, 137 pairs of tracks were purchased and issued to artillery units using Saurers as ammunition carriers. Though the idea was admirable, in practice the Delahaye tracks were more trouble than they were worth because transport and storage had to be arranged for the tracks when they were not actually on the vehicle. With the tracks fitted, top speed was reduced to 8–10 km. per hour on good surfaces.

67 **Dodge Ambulance,** 1917–19, U.S.A./U.K. and
68 **Dodge $\frac{1}{2}$-ton Light Repair Truck,** 1917–19, U.S.A./U.K.

With American entry into the war came the demand for huge numbers of extra vehicles to equip the expanding Army. Dodge Bros. had started to produce cars in 1914 and they soon got a reputation for rugged dependability. The U.S. Army bought 250 Dodge cars for use in the Mexican campaign of 1915–16 and when they became caught up in the war against Germany further orders were placed. A total of 1,012 Dodge ½-ton trucks were ordered and delivered by November 1918, these being equipped with tools and light lifting gear for limited repair work. A similar number were turned out as plain pick-ups. The repair trucks were mainly used for motor repairs. The Dodge lightweight commercial chassis was used as a basis. A smaller number of ambulances were produced on this chassis, differing only in body style. These Dodge vehicles were used by U.S. troops in both America and Europe, while the same types were purchased outright for British use.

69 Ford Model T Light Patrol Car, 1915–19, U.S.A./U.K.

The famous Ford Model T was one of the most widely used vehicles of the First World War. The British alone used about 19,000, and Model Ts were also used by the U.S. Army. The earliest Fords in service were used as ambulances only, as Henry Ford refused to let his cars be used in combat conditions, but later they were used in open tourer and saloon form as staff and liaison cars, as light trucks, and as light vans. The most famous role of all for the Model T, however, was as a light patrol car in the Western Desert and in operations against the Turks in Palestine and Mesopotamia. The Fords were first used by the Duke of Westminster's R.N.A.S. Armoured Car Squadron in the North African desert when operations were conducted in late 1915 against the German-backed Senussi who threatened Egypt from Libya. The armoured car squadron comprised a mixture of true armoured cars and some

Ford Model Ts armed with machine-guns. Because of their lighter weight the Model Ts actually proved the more successful for operating in the sand, the armoured cars frequently becoming bogged. Operations against the Senussi lasted until February 1917 when effective resistance came to an end. A detailed account of all the work done by the Model Ts in the Senussi operations is beyond the scope of this book, but this campaign in the desert was the first ever to be conducted almost entirely by motor vehicles. In a typically daring sortie a large patrol of cars penetrated 120 miles behind Senussi lines to rescue some captured British seamen held at Bir Hakkim.

Ford T light patrol cars played a vital part in the Gaza battles of 1917, impressing General Allenby, the British commander, who increased the number in service. In the advance into Palestine the light car patrols were engaged in raiding and reconnaissance and in supporting the cavalry. Six similar vehicles, armed with Lewis guns, were used (among others) by Lawrence of Arabia's armoured car force supporting the 'Arab Revolt', but it was in the Mesopotamia campaign that the Model T was used in the largest numbers. Several hundreds were used—chosen because they were the most rugged and reliable type available—and this was the first campaign to use motorised infantry extensively, the Model Ts providing the transport. A total of 300 of these vehicles was organised in a mobile group with two half-battalions of infantry plus machine-gun sections and engineers. Machine-gun detachments were also formed, with 32 Lewis guns and 150 men transported in 50 Model Ts.

The illustration shows one of the Model Ts as used in Mesopotamia. These 7-cwt vehicles were rated at 20 h.p. and had the standard Model T feature of a two speed pedal-operated gearbox. The tilt was not always fitted over the driving position. The Model Ts gave invaluable service in desert conditions, operating miles from maintenance facilities with much ingenuity and 'cannibalisation' of other vehicles, sometimes needed to keep cars running.

70 Ford Model T Rail Tractor, 1916–18, U.K.

One of the more unusual special motor vehicles developed from the Ford Model T was this rail tractor which was used on the Western Front in 1917 and 1918 on ammunition supply duties. A number of these vehicles were built, based on the engine, drive, and other components of the Model T but fitted with flanged 2 ft 3 in. gauge wheels. The terrain on the Western Front swiftly degenerated into a muddy ploughed-up waste after a few months of almost static warfare. Communication was often difficult and a large network of narrow-gauge railways was built to carry up supplies and ammunition to distribution points just behind the front line.

71 White Reconnaissance Car, 1917–19, U.S.A. and
72 White Observation Car, 1917–19, U.S.A.

Another important American type which was widely used was the White 1-tonner. The two most distinctive versions were the reconnaissance car and the observation car; 1,081 of the former were built and 1,175 of the latter, both

on the standard 1-ton White truck chassis. The only differences were in the body styles. There was also a machine-gun carrier which was almost identical in appearance to the reconnaissance car except that the rear seats were replaced by racks for ammunition. Despite its designation, incidentally, the observation car was mainly used as a staff car for divisional officers; it was equipped with map boards and signal gear.

73 2½-ton Tractor, 1918–19, U.S.A. and
74 5-ton Tractor, 1918–19, U.S.A.

The U.S. Ordnance Department ordered a whole range of tracked tractors for artillery haulage. Five sizes of tractor were considered necessary, of 2½-ton, 5-ton, 10-ton, 15-ton, and 20-ton capacity respectively. Of these, the 15-tonner was the Holt machine which had already been purchased in quantity by the British (Plate 47), and the U.S. Army bought 267 of them. The 20-tonner was also a Holt and 1,165 were ordered, though only 126 had been delivered when hostilities ceased and the order was cancelled. The smaller tractors were all designed by the Ordnance Department at Rock Island Arsenal and built under contract by commercial tractor producers. Only 10 of the 2½-ton model had been completed when the war ended, however, though more than 5,000 were initially ordered. The 5-tonner was in production first, in Summer 1918, and 1,543 were built of the 11,150 ordered. Tracked cargo trailers were contemplated, but the war ended before they were produced. It was also planned to produce self-propelled gun versions of all the tractors, with 3-inch guns mounted on

the $2\frac{1}{2}$- and 5-ton machines. The prototypes were completed, one of which is
shown in SP gun form, and 270 were
ordered. However, after the Armistice
production was cancelled.

75 A7V Überlandwagen, 1917–18, Germany

This unusual supply carrier was built on
the chassis of the famous German A7V
Sturmpanzerwagen, the first and only
German tank to see operational service
in the First World War. The A7V was
produced in 1917 following the British
and French use of tanks. In the A7V,
twin Daimler 100-h.p. engines were
mounted side by side in the centre with a
control position, arranged for drive in
either direction, placed on a platform
above the engines. The suspension was
derived from the Holt tractor suspension, the American tractor which had
also provided the early inspiration for
British and French tanks. The A7V
Sturmpanzerwagen had a box-like
enveloping superstructure but when it
was first conceived the design committee made allowance for the chassis to
be fitted with an alternative load carrier
body. A total of 30 A7V Überland-
wagens (as the supply carrier version
was called) was projected but not all
were completed before the war ended.
In the Überlandwagen a canopy was
provided over the central control position and wood dropsides and ends were
fitted fore and aft of the engine compartment. In some vehicles rails were added
(as shown) to support a tarpaulin cover
over the load spaces. The vehicle had a
top speed of 8 m.p.h. and was crewed by
a driver and one assistant. The seats in
the control position swivelled and the

controls were duplicated for driving in
either direction without the need for
turning. Tow hooks were fitted at both
ends of the chassis. The A7V Überlandwagen was in service on the Western
Front from May-June 1918 and contemporary pictures show them carrying
general stores and ammunition up to
front line positions. Some vehicles
operated with the dropsides removed,
leaving just a flatbed platform. The
vehicle was 26 ft long and 10 ft wide.

76 Riker 3-ton Lorry, 1917–18, U.S.A./U.K.

Aside from the Dodge (Plate 68) and
Jeffery-Quad (Plate 50) the British
Government bought several other well-
known makes of truck from America.
These included Macks, Whites, Kelly-
Springfields, Packards (Plate 31) and
Rikers. One of the latter is shown here,
displaying yet another special-purpose
body which resulted from the prevailing
conditions of the First World War. This
is a water purification plant operated at
water supply points by the Royal
Engineers. The plant filtered (and made
provision for testing) water taken from
local sources, and was an important item
of equipment on the Western Front
where normal fresh water supplies were
disrupted and usually suspect.

77 Commer Ambulance, 1916–18, U.K.

Commercial Cars Ltd. of Luton did not
produce any designs to meet the War
Office subsidy requirements, but none-
theless the urgent need for transport led
the British Army to order the standard
Commer chassis/cab for use in special
non-combatant roles. They were not

used for troop or supply carrying but were fitted with specialist bodywork for less demanding functions. Illustrated is a Commer First Aid lorry which carried medical stores and stretchers, etc, to supply first aid posts; it also operated forward from casualty clearing stations as a mobile first aid post itself, complete with medical officer or medical attendants. Other Commer chassis of this type were fitted with horsebox bodies and some of these were further modified as horse ambulances. The horsebox/horse ambulance body was van-like but with slatted upper sides; it could carry two horses and had a full-depth door in the near side which dropped to form a loading ramp for the animals. There was a central partition running fore-and-aft which formed two stalls inside. The horse ambulance version carried extra veterinary stores, and slings and tackle for moving injured animals. The Commer had a 25-h.p. four-cylinder engine and a Lindley gearbox which was a primitive form of the pre-selector type. It had chain final drives which were carried in enclosed casings.

78 Crossley Staff Car, 1918, U.K.

The Crossley was used exclusively by the Royal Flying Corps, and its successor the Royal Air Force. Basically derived from the standard Crossley car, the RFC/RAF type car was modified slightly for service use with twin rear wheels and stronger springs. This vehicle is shown with its WAAF driver in 1918 uniform.

79 Crossley Tender, 1918, U.K.

This was a variant on the same chassis as the staff car shown in Plate 78. The

tender was produced in much greater numbers than the staff car for use in general service on airfields. Crossley built over 4,000 vehicles for the RFC/RAF in the years 1915–18.

80 F.W.D. Model B 3-ton Lorry, 1916–18, U.S.A./U.K.

To make up for their drastic shortage of motor transport the British Government purchased huge numbers of motor vehicles from the United States, a total of nearly 18,000 being thus acquired during the war years. First contracts were placed at the end of 1914 and first deliveries of vehicles were made early in 1915 via an American export agency which set up a reception base in Liverpool and a repair depot in Islington to check and service incoming vehicles before handing them over to the British Ministry of Munitions. Only the cab/chassis came from America, the British fitting W.D.-type bodies of their own as required. One of the most important types purchased was the F.W.D. Model B, built by the Four Wheel Drive Co. of Clintonville, Wisconsin, from whence the F.W.D. initials were derived. As its name implies, this was a four-wheel drive vehicle and very similar to its contemporary the Jeffrey-Quad (Plate 50). Rated as a 3-tonner, the F.W.D. had a Wisconsin four-cylinder petrol engine with a three-speed gearbox and a two-speed transfer gearbox. There was a shaft drive to each axle. On roads the F.W.D. was driven as a normal rear-wheel drive vehicle, but for off-road driving an additional gear lever was provided on the chassis side which controlled the low gears and connected up the drive to the front axle. In the

British Army the F.W.D. was mainly used as a gun tractor but it also saw service as a supply carrier for heavy or awkward loads. A typical role saw it fitted with a tank for carrying petrol or water as in the vehicle illustrated. This particular example was in service on the Italian front in 1916.

81 **F.W.D. Artillery Supply Truck,** 1917–18, U.S.A.
82 **F.W.D. Artillery Repair Truck,** 1917–18, U.S.A.
83 **F.W.D. Ordnance Repair Truck,** 1917–18, U.S.A.
84 **Jeffrey 240-mm. Mortar Carrier,** 1918, U.S.A.

The British and French had purchased four-wheel drive vehicles like the F.W.D., Nash, Jeffery-Quad, and Knox from American firms from the earliest days of the war. When the Americans entered the war in April 1917, they too ordered four-wheel drive vehicles in quantity, mainly F.W.D. Nash and Jeffery makes. The U.S. Ordnance Department had the benefit of nearly three years observation of the war in France and an early decision was taken to avoid the use of horse-drawn artillery equipment in the American Expeditionary Force as much as possible. Thus the Americans went to war from the start with the emphasis on mechanical rather than horse-drawn transport. No less than 30,000 four-wheel drive vehicles were ordered of which 12,498 had been delivered by the time of the Armistice. Of these 9,420 went to France before hostilities ceased. A complete range of complementary bodies was produced (25,000 in total) for fitting to the F.W.D. chassis and a selection of these are shown.

They were almost entirely steel in contrast with the British range of W.D. bodies (in Plate 80 for example) which were wood. The artillery supply truck carried ammunition and gun spares and 5,474 were ordered. The artillery repair truck carried lathes, welding plant, riveting equipment, and so on for gun repairs in the field and over 1,300 of these were ordered. The ordnance repair truck was for general repair work embracing such items as motor vehicles, wagons, and even horse harness. The final illustration in this group (Plate 84) shows a body designed specifically to carry the very heavy 240-mm. (10-inch) trench mortar. This weapon suffered from design problems, and consequent production delays however, and only 24 mortars were completed. The weapon, and its carrier, were not used in action, but the illustration affords a good contrast between the Jeffery chassis (see also Plate 50) and the F.W.D.

85 **Liberty Four-Wheel Drive Truck,** 1916–18, U.S.A./U.K.

As recounted in more detail below, the U.S. Ordnance Department determined from an early stage that standardisation was desirable for the mass-production of the huge numbers of trucks needed to put the U.S. Army on its planned war footing. The F.W.D., Jeffery, and Nash four-wheel drive vehicles were regarded as interim types and plans went ahead to produce a so-called 'Liberty' version to standardised design. The prototype, which virtually incorporated features from all the different individual makes of four-wheel drive vehicles, was completed in late 1918 and is shown with the standard ammunition supply body;

the other specialist bodies could also be fitted. With the cessation of hostilities this vehicle never went into production and the F.W.D. remained the most numerous type in service with the U.S. Army for many years afterwards.

86 Liberty Class B 5-ton Truck (converted to six wheels), 1919, U.S.A.

America entered the First World War in April 1917 and a U.S. Expeditionary Force was sent to Europe. A massive build-up was promised by 1919 and America started a huge armaments (and recruiting) programme to provide the necessary forces. Motor transport on a big scale was required for the greatly expanded U.S. Army and it was originally planned that the Society of Automotive Engineers—the trade organisation of American truck manufacturers—would set up a committee to work out a production programme and lay down a standard truck specification to which all manufacturers would conform (within agreed limits for individual differences). This scheme came to nothing, however, since most firms had their own ideas for interpreting the specifications which did not always fit in with service requirements. With nothing decided, the U.S. Government stepped in, in July 1917, and insisted on a rigidly standardised 'war truck' design to which all manufacturers had to work. Thus was born the famous Liberty truck. (There was also a Liberty aero engine which was a similar standardised design).

The initial requirement was for a

3½-ton truck and production had to be under way within 6 months. The S.A.E. committee specification was used as a basis but the finished design was really a 'mongrel' which used parts based on designs by most of the major engine and chassis manufacturers. Two prototypes were running within 30 days of the requirement being announced, such was the urgency of the programme. The engine was a 60-h.p. four-cylinder unit with Wankesha cylinders, Hercules pistons, Wankesha governor, and so on. The back axle was from Timken and Sheldon parts. This was a fully floating unit with worm drive. Steel spoked wheels with solid tyres were used though early vehicles had wooden wheels.

As a stopgap until the Liberty truck was in full production the U.S. Government ordered 100,000 commercial trucks for military service from Packard, Pierce-Arrow, Riker, F.W.D., Nash and Garford. Examples of some of these —which were already being supplied to Britain and, (in some cases) France, are illustrated elsewhere in this book. Over 24,000 lorry bodies were also ordered, some for the commercial trucks and the rest for the Liberty trucks.

Once the 3½-ton Liberty was finalised, requirements for two other types were formulated. One was for a 15-cwt light truck, the Liberty Class AA, and the other was for a 5-ton heavy truck similar to the original 3½-ton design but with the wheelbase extended to 160½ in. and bigger tyres. Twin tyres (40 in.) were fitted at the rear and were of the press-on type. Chassis had pressed channel steel frames and the four-cylinder motor had three point suspension. There were four forward speeds and reverse, with Hotchkiss final drive. Lubrication was revised and all moving parts drew oil by capillary action along wicks from adjacent lubrication points.

The Liberty scheme was, in the event, much better on paper than in practice. The manufacturers were too busy on the new U.S. Army contracts to build Liberty trucks initially and aspects of the original Liberty design needed modifying—they were corrected in the Class B. Essentially the original Liberty had been based on the experience of the Mexican war of 1916 where roads were bad or non-existent. So the gearing was too elaborate for France where roads were generally good and little or no off-road running was required. Thus the Liberty scheme was revised and the $3\frac{1}{2}$-ton and Class AA models were abandoned and only Class B, re-rated as a 3-tonner, was retained. Contracts for 8,000 Class B trucks were placed on 25 May 1918 with 16 companies including Packard, Sheldon, Garford, and Kelly-Springfield. Unit price per truck was just over £100. By early July, 2,500 Class Bs had been delivered and production had reached 75 vehicles a day. By the time of the Armistice the U.S. Army had 62,375 vehicles altogether of which 32,500 were lorries, more being commercial types than Liberty Class Bs.

The illustration shows a Liberty Class B in post-war years when it had been converted to a rigid six-wheeler with a Goodyear-Templin rear bogie replacing the original back axle. This had a single axle with a sprocket and chain drive to the inside of the rear wheels. Dating from 1920, it was the first six-wheeler in U.S. Army service. The standard Liberty Class B was similar in appearance except for its single rear wheels.

87 **Liberty Class C 5-ton Truck,** 1920, U.S.A.
and
88 **Liberty Class C chassis,** 1920, U.S.A.

The conversion of the Liberty Class B (Plate 86) to six-wheel configuration led to a modernisation of the existing Liberty vehicles to give improved performance. The Goodyear-Templin tandem bogie was fitted in place of the original rear axle and new wheels with pneumatic tyres were fitted all round. Finally a new cab with side doors was added and the vehicle was re-rated as a 5-tonner. Thus modernised it was known as the Liberty Class C and many of these vehicles remained in U.S. Army service until just before the Second World War.

89 **F.W.D. Model B Ordnance Maintenance Truck,** 1920, U.S.A.

The U.S. Army had first improvised repair trucks in the Mexican Border operations in 1916. In France in 1917–18 some mobile repair shops based on the current British type had been used by artillery regiments of the American Expeditionary Forces pending availability of the F.W.D. types (Plates 80 and 81). It was not until 1920, that the U.S. Army had its F.W.D. ordnance maintenance trucks in widespread service. A typical Ordnance Company had three F.W.D. trucks each fitted up with generator, anvil, lathe, and drilling equipment. Ten ordinary F.W.D. trucks carried tools, spares, and stock-bins. The 32nd Ordnance Company supported a big mobility exercise in September 1921 when a complete heavy artillery regiment and an engineer unit with a total of 240 trucks, and 38 tractors, and big guns made a 600-mile, 40-day run from Camp Jackson, South Carolina, to Camp Eustis, Virginia, arriving with all vehicles intact and serviceable thanks to the accompanying workshop facilities of the Ordnance Company.

The illustration shows one of the vehicles as it appeared during the exercise. It is changed in detail from the original 1918 model. The U.S. Army made extensive use of F.W.D. trucks for many years—the F.W.D. was known as the 'Flirt With Death' to the U.S. troops.

90 **Citroen-Kegresse prototype,** 1923, France

91 **Citroen-Kegresse Line-Layer,** 1925, U.K.

92 **Burford-Kegresse Artillery Tractor,** 1926, U.K.

93 **Burford-Kegresse Truck,** 1926, U.K.

For several years after 1918 the British Army made do with a motley collection of transport vehicles left over from the war. Everything from subsidy 3-tonners to American F.W.D.s and other types remained in service, while ex-RAF Crossley tenders (Plate 79) were also taken into Army stock. The most inventive progress was made in France with Renault and Citroen making all the running. In 1921 a novel semi-tracked version of the Citroen car appeared utilising rubber band track units and bogies in place of the rear wheels. This track system was the brainchild of Adolphe Kegresse who had been transport manager to the Russian Czar prior to the 1917 Revolution.

While in the Czar's employ Kegresse had perfected his half-track system as early as 1910, specifically to make the Czar's cars run better in the snow. With the Revolution, Kegresse left Russia and returned to France via Finland. In Paris he offered his track unit design to Andre Citroen. Citroen's first 10-h.p. Citroen-Kegresse was tested in the Alps with great success and in 1922–23 the type enjoyed huge publicity when an expedition equipped with these vehicles made the first crossing of the Sahara Desert by the motor car. The Citroen-Kegresse (which had the usual Citroen 'traction-avante') was adopted in large numbers by the French Army, and about eight vehicles of this type were purchased by the British Army in 1924–26. They were known as 'Citroen-Kegresse Battery Staff Cars' to the British, though two were later fitted to tow 3·7-inch howitzers on tracked trailers. The first vehicle in service was adapted as a signals line-layer, being fitted at the rear with a standard Royal Engineers cable laying wagon which was normally horse-drawn. This is the vehicle illustrated. It caused something of a sensation in the 1925 Autumn manoeuvres by travelling cross-country at will laying telephone cables, a task hitherto carried out by horse detachments. While Britain purchased no more Citroens, a number of Crossley and Burford lorries were converted to Kegresse half-track configuration and were used with great success, the Burfords finding employment as gun tractors (Plate 92), and as load carriers (Plate 93). The Citroen-Kegresse was historically a most important type providing the inspiration for the German and American half-tracks of World War 2.

94 **Morris-Roadless 1-ton Truck,**
1926, U.K. and
95 **Guy-Roadless 1-ton Truck,**
1926, U.K.

The Citroen-Kegresse soon inspired others. In Britain a brilliant tank designer of World War 1, Lt-Col. P. Johnson, who had been responsible for the very advanced Medium Mark D tanks, left the Army in 1923 when his Tank Design Department was wound up as an economy measure. Johnson took his expertise into the commercial world and formed the Roadless Traction Co. One of his first projects was to design a track unit on the lines of the Kegresse idea which could replace the rear wheels of tractors or cars. It differed considerably from the rubber-tracked Kegresse product, however. The track shoes were all steel but were fully flexible and were longitudinally sprung, a feature of the so-called 'Snake' tracks which Johnson had earlier used for his tank designs (see Plate 101). This was an efficient system for the track adjusted itself to surface contours, especially when steering through a curve, instead of just skidding over the surface. Silent running was achieved by rubber tyres on the sprocket and idler wheels. The Roadless track units were designed so that the sprocket wheel (the largest wheel) fitted directly on the rear axle hub in the place of the normal wheel, while the idler wheels were supported by the brackets added to the chassis frames. The small road wheels were carried on an arm pivoted from the idler axle. Almost any lorry could be fitted up with Roadless tracks and the conversion from wheels to track and vice versa could be carried out in a couple of hours. Guy and Morris

1-ton trucks were the first to be converted and offered for sale in 1924 and 1925 respectively. The British Army purchased six Guys and three Morris vehicles, two with a 14-h.p. and one with a 16-h.p. engine. The first of these is shown (Plate 94) and this was fitted up as a machine-gun carrier. It had a demountable pintle mount (not shown) in the centre of the rear load space and this could be fitted with a Lewis gun. The other two vehicles were used as normal load carriers. All three were basically specifically designed for military use. These vehicles were disposed of in 1933. No more Morris-Roadless vehicles were bought but similar conversions of old F.W.D.s were used in some numbers. The Roadless track unit also formed the running gear for the famous Morris-Martel tankettes which attracted much attention in the twenties. In many ways the Roadless track unit was technically superior to the Kegresse though it never achieved the same fame. A speed of 12–15 m.p.h. could be safely attained with Roadless tracks though faster speeds were possible in practice. Plate 95 shows the Guy 1-tonner which acted as prototype and demonstration vehicle for the Roadless series.

96 **Renault 12-cwt Dragon,** 1926, France/U.K.

Not to be outdone by Citroen who gained valuable publicity from the Citroen-Kegresse Sahara crossing of 1922, Louis Renault produced a six-wheel car in 1923 based on the standard 13·9-h.p. Renault chassis but with an extra rear axle. Rear drive was via a transfer box mounted above the foremost axle driving direct and to the rear axle by a flexibly-coupled shaft. In December 1923 this Renault car, fitted with twin wheels and pneumatic tyres on each axle, bettered Citroen's feat by making the first Sahara crossing by a fully *wheeled* vehicle, in only five days, covering 2,000 miles. The Renault Desert Car, as it was called, was offered for sale as a cross-country vehicle. The British War Office borrowed one for tests, which took place in March 1924. Results were impressive and ultimately led to the British decision to adopt six-wheelers rather than half-tracks for future motor transport needs. On the War Office trials the Renault made a long climb—including stops and starts —up a 1 in 10 gradient at an average 10 m.p.h. It ran unladen up a 1 in $3\frac{3}{4}$ gradient, crossed sand, and ran over marshland, all with ease. The War Office subsequently purchased a chassis outright and fitted it with a W.D. type body for use as a gun tractor or Dragon. From 1924–28 it was used extensively for service trials by 'P' Company R.A.S.C. at Aldershot, and is illustrated as it appeared at that time, complete with full seating for the gun's crew. No further orders for Renaults were placed by the British, but experience with this vehicle greatly influenced future requirements formulated for motor transport.

From 1925 the French also put a few vehicles of this type into service. The Renault Dragon was 14 ft long, 6 ft 3 in. wide, and had a 10 ft 3 in. wheelbase. It had three speeds in two combinations; there was a four-cylinder engine and the vehicle boasted the familiar Renault features of a 'coal scuttle' bonnet and radiator behind the engine. Body length

was $9\frac{1}{2}$ ft. Speeds of up to 30 m.p.h. were possible.

97 **T.T.S.W. 1$\frac{1}{2}$-ton Truck,** 1926, U.S.A.

The first U.S. Army six-wheel drive vehicle appeared in 1924 and was designed by the Engineering Section of the Motor Transport Division. This vehicle used some Liberty truck components to keep costs down (much war surplus Liberty material was to hand) but mechanically it was almost completely new. A four-cylinder Hinkley engine was used. Drive was via a Covert clutch to a four-speed gearbox with a shaft to an auxiliary gearbox between the chassis frames behind the cab. A shaft drove the back axle with drive to the rear axle via a shaft with two universal joints. Suspension of the rear bogie was by semi-elliptic springs and telescopic torque members. The torque members were pivoted about the vertical axis and allowed the two axles to move relative to each other when the springs were flexed. Drive for the front axle was also via a shaft from the auxiliary gearbox, and a further shaft drove a winch located beneath the chassis side members. Bonnet, cab, mudguards, body, etc, were all Liberty parts. The vehicle was rated as a 3-tonner and a four-wheel version, similar except for the single rear axle, was rated as a 2-tonner. The SW type was a major advance on the old Liberty vehicles. Interesting features included an adjustable steering wheel and fully-enclosed band brakes on the rear wheel hubs which ran in oil to reduce wear and remain waterproof. There were also transmission brakes. The version of the SW illustrated is an experimental version of the SW type produced in 1926 with twin wheels on each axle. Known as the T.T.S.W. (twin-tyre, six-wheeler) it differed from the standard model in having twin wheels on each axle to further improve traction. The rear bogie was known as the Goodyear-Templin type after the firms which perfected and built it.

98 Dragon Mark I Gun Tractor, 1924, U.K.

The usefulness of the Holt tractor in the war years led the Royal Artillery to adopt purpose-built crawler track tractors in the 'twenties. Known as a 'Dragon', a corruption of 'drag gun', this type of vehicle was developed by Vickers concurrently with the Vickers Light (later Medium) tank which was produced to the requirements of the Master General of the Ordnance. The Dragon provided seating for the gun crew and carried spare ammunition and battery equipment. Illustrated is the Dragon Mark I which appeared in 1922 and was in service a couple of years later. It had similar 'box bogie' suspension and chassis units to the Vickers Medium tank and was of similar overall dimensions. It had a Leyland four-cylinder 60-h.p. engine, weighed 9 tons, and had a top speed of 12 m.p.h. on the road. It carried 10 men and held 64 rounds of field gun ammunition. It towed the standard 18-pdr. gun and limber, replacing the horse team hitherto used with this weapon.

99 Dragon Mark II Gun Tractor, 1926, U.K.

The tracked Dragon design was continually improved during the twenties and thirties. The Mark II first appeared in 1923, notably differentiated from its previous models by the improved crew and engine protection afforded by the fully enclosed superstructure. The chassis was altered only in detail but to give a better performance (16 m.p.h.) an Armstrong-Siddeley 82-h.p. V8 engine was fitted. The Mark II Dragon was in service in the 1925 manoeuvres for the first time. It proved to have a less satisfactory hauling power than the Mark I so more were subsequently altered to Mark II★ with reduced final drive and strengthened steering clutches. As a gun tractor for 18-pdrs. the Dragon II/II★ carried 11 men and 128 rounds of field gun ammunition. The illustration shows a vehicle modified in 1926 to act as battery wireless link complete with primitive service radio of the period. This is a very early example of a radio-fitted command vehicle, though not in fact the first.

100a and 100b Vickers-Wolseley Staff Car, 1926, U.K.

The twenties were a period of experiment in military vehicles, especially on the problem of preserving track life. Alternative wheel and track propulsion was postulated by Vickers, with wheels being used for road running and tracks across country. In 1923 they altered a Wolseley touring car. Variously called a wheel-and-track staff car or a reconnaissance car, this vehicle had track assemblies running in vertical guides. The tracks were lowered from a power take off, using bell-crank arms. The vehicle was demonstrated to Colonial governors along with other recent military equipment after the Colonial Conference of May 1927. It caused a sensation at the time but the idea was largely impracticable and also unstable. The following year Vickers used the same wheel-and-track arrangement on a tank and it seems probable that they regarded the Wolseley merely as a cheap test vehicle to try out the idea—it proved even less successful applied to a tank.

101 **Light D Tank,** 1923, U.K.

One of the most unusual of all military vehicles the Light 'D' was a purely experimental type built by Lt-Col. P. Johnson who was in the years 1918–21 a prominent tank designer. He was an advocate of the high-speed tank with sprung, flexible tracks, ideas far in advance of his contemporaries. Johnson was responsible for the ingenious but ill-fated Medium 'D' tank produced in 1919, and afterwards he continued his design work with projects or prototypes for tropical, light infantry, and light tanks. The Light 'D' was a development vehicle for the latter class and utilised a normal Ruston car chassis with its wheels replaced by tracks. The spring bogies can be seen and the track shoes also pivoted laterally as they moved over irregular surfaces. This gave a better, smoother, ride than on most previous British tanks which had unsprung tracks. Johnson's ideas were, in fact, well ahead of their time and his projects were all abandoned in the post-war defence cuts of the early twenties. Johnson later left the Army and set up the Roadless Traction Co., still a well-known commercial firm. (see Plates 94 and 95).

102a and 102b **Pavesi P4,** 1913, Italy/France

103 **Pavesi Gun Tractor,** 1926, Italy

104 **Pavesi Tractor Mark I,** 1926, U.K.

One of the earliest vehicles capable of four-wheel drive cross-country work was the Pavesi tractor, originally an agricultural machine, first produced by the firm of Pavesi-Tolotti of Milan in 1913. This ingenious machine depended for its remarkably good cross-country performance on an articulated chassis so that the front and rear ends could move laterally and vertically almost independently of each other as is apparent from the chassis drawing. There was a front-mounted engine, and drive to the rear wheel was by double-jointed universal shaft with bevel gearing. Large diameter wheels were fitted and a variety of types—steel-studded, solid-tyred, double, etc—were offered to suit customers' requirements. In 1914 senior French officers watched a demonstration of the machine's abilities and were impressed enough to seek further details. However, when war came interest in such out of the way types was shelved.

In the twenties military interest in the capabilities of the Pavesi tractor were revived. The Italian Army tested some vehicles fitted with armoured bodies and turrets—they were popularly known as the 'Pavesi Wheeled Tank'—using the model P4 chassis, then the latest in the Pavesi range. From 1926 the P4 type, now produced by Fiat who had bought up the original firm, was used widely by the Italian Army as a gun tractor, and one of these is shown in Plate 103 with a 75-mm. howitzer detachment. A few of these vehicles were still in use in the Second World War. The P4 had a 50-h.p. Pavesi four-cylinder engine, weighed about 4 tons, and could tow just over 3 tons. In Britain from 1923 Armstrong-Siddeley had the agency for Pavesi tractors and built some under licence. They tried to interest the British Army in this type of vehicle. Between 1924–30, however, the military authorities purchased only three and borrowed two others for trials. One of these vehicles is shown in Plate 104. It has a plain open box body differing from the type used on the Italian Pavesi. A few other Pavesi tractors were used in Britain by firms specialising in hiring out vehicles to military and other authorities for contract work. The internally sprung wheel is of interest. A further option in the P4 vehicle was pneumatic tyres.

105 **Karrier WO6 Medium Lorry,** 1926, U.K.
106 **Crossley 3-ton Medium Lorry,** 1926, U.K.

The first British rigid six-wheeler design was the Karrier WO6 which was produced in 1924, directly influenced by the Goodyear-Templin ideas for rigid six-wheelers in U.S.A. (Plate 97) and the success of the Renault six-wheeler (Plate 96). Design started in June and the prototype was ready in November. The firm of Guy Motors was concurrently working on a similar six-wheel design. In February 1925 there was a further War Office trial which included a comparison of the Renault with the Karrier and the Guy. The Karrier WO6 had a four-cylinder 48-h.p. engine. There was a four-speed and reverse gearbox, plus an auxiliary gearbox with two speeds,

giving both direct drive and a 3:1 reduction on all gears. Thus in effect there were eight forward speeds and two reverse speeds, though in practice the main gearbox only was used on roads with the auxiliary gearbox brought in for cross-country or other rough going. The rear bogie, which like the Renault had both rear axles driven, had overhead worm drive with a pivoted tube between the axles enclosing the two universal joints and the shaft. Radius rods joined the worm casing on each axle to a central cross member. The springs were inverted semi-elliptics, pivoted centrally between the axles, a similar arrangement to that of the Renault six-wheeler. The two rear-driven axles thus had independent articulation both laterally and longitudinally to allow them to follow the ground contours without excessive displacement of the chassis and without losing ground contact. This, of course, had also been the secret of the Renault's success for traction was constantly maintained over almost any cross-country surface.

In 1923 the War Office had formulated a new subsidy scheme for 30-cwt lorries with normal rear-wheel drive (what later became known as 4 × 2 type) and Karrier (Plate 105), Crossley (Plate 106), Albion, and Talbot had produced vehicles to meet the necessary specification. The performance of the new Karrier and Guy six-wheelers with twin rear bogie drive at the 1925 War Office trial was so impressive, however, that little time was lost in modifying the subsidy scheme to include this type of vehicle. Meanwhile, the Mechanical Transport Department encouraged manufacturers to develop rigid six-wheelers and drew up various necessary conditions based on experience with the Renault and Karrier. The rear driving wheels had to bear equal weight under any conditions, the suspension had to be freely articulated without twisting the springs or displacing the chassis, there was to be some way of preventing skid and providing optimum adhesion on soft ground, while a small engine geared down was deemed preferable to a large one. The M.T.D.'s experimental branch duly designed a standard form of rear bogie and suspension, very similar to that of the Karrier, and also designed and patented simple chain tracks which would slip over the two rear wheels when conditions demanded, so turning the vehicle into a rudimentary half-track. Twin rear wheels were in fact, specified for military use and the track fitted neatly between the tyres. Each chain-link track weighed $1\frac{1}{2}$ cwt and was normally carried in a special stowage on the chassis. These tracks became standard on all British military six-wheelers for the next twenty years or so. Demonstrations of prototypes built on the lines suggested were held in October 1926 at Chobham Ridges, a rugged and testing military exercise area. The Karrier and Guy plus a Thornycroft and a light Morris, all rigid six-wheelers took part. In May 1927 a new subsidy scheme for 'Medium W.D.-Type Six-Wheelers' was duly announced, worth £120 over three years. Karrier (with the WO6) Guy, Crossley, Albion and Thornycroft were among qualifying firms who produced designs and they of course supplied vehicles of the same type direct

to the Army. Apart from the suspension and drive system (which allowed detail variations) and body and overall dimensions, the subsidy scheme was flexible enough to allow normal or forward control. The medium class was rated at $2-3\frac{1}{2}$ tons, the latter being the military rating.

Among the first commercial firms to purchase the subsidy type Karriers of the WO6 design was the Artillery Transport Co. Ltd. of York who eventually had 24 of them, one of which is shown in the illustration. This company was formed by an artillery officer, Captain Riley. In the twenties when military expenditure was cut to a minimum there was rarely sufficient transport available when it was most required, so for big exercises it was the practice to hire suitable vehicles locally. The Territorial Army, in particular, invariably had to resort to hiring for their annual camps. Riley's idea was to set up a fleet which could be equipped with military-type vehicles and hired out specifically for army manoeuvres. He chose the Karriers because they could accommodate a complete 18-pdr. field gun and limber and transport them *portée*-fashion across country, a much quicker procedure than towing. The illustration (Plate 105) shows this method. The equipment could, of course, be towed in the normal way. In winter or other non-exercise periods, Riley hired out his vehicles to farmers and others like the Forestry Commission who needed cross-country transport. The War Department Karriers were identical to the vehicle shown except in body detail.

107a **Morris-Commercial D Type Light Lorry**, 1928, U.K.
107b **WD patent articulating rear bogie**, 1928, U.K.
108 **Morris-Commercial D Type Wireless Van**, 1928, U.K.
109 **Morris-Commercial CD Type**, 1932, U.K.

In February 1928 the subsidy scheme for a 'Light WD Type Six-wheeler Lorry' was formally published which called for a rigid six-wheeler in the $1-1\frac{1}{2}$-ton class —in other words a 20–30 cwt. The requirements regarding drive and suspension were similar to those for the medium type described above. The W.D. design for a rear bogie could be used or the manufacturer was free to produce a design which matched it in performance. Forward or normal control was permitted but body dimensions were specified as 8 ft long, 2 ft 10 in. deep, and $5\frac{1}{2}$ ft wide. The normal GS (i.e. lorry) body was to be of the well type, stepped at the sides to form seats for troop carrying, Morris had already produced a prototype broadly to these requirements and this had participated in the 1926 trials. Morris-Commercial with their 'Light D' model now became the major producer of this class of vehicle (though Crossley, Garner and Vulcan also made 'Light types) and hundreds were built for military, commercial, and overseas use, production continuing with detailed changes until 1939. The Morris-Commercial D Types had a four-cylinder side-valve 40-h.p. engine with the usual four-speed gear box and two speed auxiliary box. With 80:1 reduction of its lowest auxiliary gear it had a superb climbing ability cross-country, better than that of the

Medium lorries. Versions of the Morris were produced as mobile workshops, recovery vehicles, ambulances and articulated semi-trailer stores and office vehicles with the basic chassis as prime-mover. Most common was the ordinary general service truck body (Plate 107), but the drawing shows a Morris wireless van (Plate 108) as used in the Mechanised Force manoeuvres of 1927 and 1928. The radio masts were normally folded flat on the roof when not in use. In 1933 the CD Type appeared, which was simply an up-dated version of the D Type with improved cab, wheels, and body (Plate 109).

110 **Citroen P.17 Machine-Gun Carrier**, 1931, France/U.S.A.
111 **Citroen P.17 Gun Tractor**, 1931, France/U.S.A.
112 **Citroen P.14 Breakdown Truck**, 1928–32, France

Between 1927–33 the French Army was entirely mechanised and the Citroen-Kegresse half-track was widely adopted in its latest form. The three main versions are shown. The P.17 of 1931 had an 'unditching roller' on the nose and many detailed improvements over earlier models. The gun tractor shown (Plate 111) is actually that purchased by the U.S. Army in 1932 for trials, as a result of which half-track development started in America leading to the big 'family' of half-tracks produced in America in the Second World War period. It is towing an American 75-mm. gun. The same vehicle was used by the French for towing 75-mm. artillery and in this case the gun could be transported on a wheeled bogie known as train-rolleur which greatly increased the towing speed over smooth terrain. The machine-gun carrier (Plate 110) equipped the mechanised cavalry regiments and provided accommodation for a Hotchkiss machine-gun, its crew, and ammunition. The breakdown vehicle was a retrospective army modification of an older vehicle to take a jib, windlass, and winch for the recovery of other vehicles in mechanised units.

113 **Ceirano Auto-Cannone 75 mm.,** 1929, Italy

By the end of the First World War, A.A. guns had generally become too big and powerful to be fired from the normal commercial type of vehicle, and the tendency was towards towed A.A. guns. One of the last vehicles fitted with an A.A. gun in the traditional way was produced by Ceirano, a subsidiary of Fiat, in 1928 and a number of these 'Auto-Cannones' were built for the Italian Army. The gun was a 75-mm. piece suitable for A.A. or surface fire. Outriggers were fitted to stay the chassis when the gun was fired. A few of these vehicles survived to serve in the Second World War. The Italian Army also used the standard Ceirano truck without the A.A. gun as a normal load carrier.

114 **Trojan Light Six-Wheeler,** 1929, U.K.

Produced in 1929 and used in small numbers by the British Army, the Trojan light six-wheeler was a 'private venture' design with its own unique features. It had the usual Trojan two-

stroke engine of $1\frac{1}{2}$ litres and the punt-like chassis common to all Trojans, but extended rearwards by steel channel plates in order to give the increased wheelbase necessary. The bogie was of tubular construction with adjustable axles and chain drive throughout. There were two semi-elliptic leaf springs, one each side, with rubber snubbers on each axle to prevent them bearing upon the springs over exceptionally rough ground. A steel track band was provided—similar to the W.D.-type rubber track band—which could be fitted round the rear wheels to turn the vehicle into a rudimentary half-track for cross-country work. There were two alternative body styles, one accommodating six men on the seats above the wheels and a slightly longer body accommodating eight men. Mechanically the vehicle was identical to the ordinary commercial Trojan delivery van.

115 and 116 **Hathi Tractor,** 1927–33, U.K.

This vehicle was the British Army's first indigenous four-wheel drive tractor. The prototype was in fact made up from parts of captured German four-wheel drive tractors left over from the Great War and this was tested in 1923 as a towing vehicle for heavy artillery. This led to an order for a new improved model, the Hathi II, built as new. Thornycroft undertook this work, utilising an 11-litre six-cylinder marine engine to give the necessary power. The prototype Hathi II was built in 1924 and took part in War Office trials in October of that year. Drive was by means of a centrally-mounted six-speed gearbox, actually a three-speed box but with a choice of high or low ratios for each gear. In normal conditions high or low ratio was selected, then gears were changed as for a three-speed box. The engine was offset to the right, as was the gearbox, and drive shafts led fore and aft to the axles. Both axles were of conventional type but final drive to the front wheels was through hollow stub axles to allow for steering; bevelled gear wheels allowed for a flexible joint as the wheels were steered.

There was a horizontal winch-mounted on the centre line of the chassis with a worm-driven laying on device for the purchase and leads both front and back. A separate lever in the gearbox allowed the winch to be engaged by a sliding spur wheel. Transmission brakes only were fitted, the front brakes being operated by the foot pedal and the rear brakes by lever. There was a simple superstructure made up of stowage boxes, with seats for the crew. The Hathi, of which about 30 were built, was a most powerful vehicle though it suffered from poor traction on heavy slippery mud surfaces. To improve performance in these conditions, tyre-chains were carried and portable wooden scotches could be placed under the wheels to facilitate winching.

Hathi tractors were used well into the thirties, both in Britain and India, though those vehicles shipped overseas had deeper radiators fitted. One or two vehicles were converted to heavy re-covery vehicles with added jibs, and another vehicle (Plate 116) was experimentally converted to six-wheel drive by the addition of a W.D. pattern twin rear bogie. This vehicle had twin wheels fitted, giving a total of twelve wheels and six-wheel drive. The Hathi was mainly used as a towing vehicle for 60-pdr. or 6-inch guns.

117 F.W.D. Gun Tractor, 1932, U.K.

The American F.W.D. Model B Trac-tor had given yeoman service to the Allies both during and after the First World War (Plates 80 to 83). In Britain after the war the British F.W.D. Tractor Lorry Co. was formed as agents for this vehicle, many of which remained in Britain after being sold off as war sur-plus. Later the firm became the F.W.D. Lorry Co. with works at Slough. In 1927–28 the British Army drew up requirements for a third type of subsidy vehicle in the 'Heavy' class rated at 3–4 tons. Though nothing came of this, it coincided with the appearance of a 6-ton six-wheel drive rigid six-wheeler from F.W.D. In mid-1928, the War Depart-ment ordered one of these vehicles for test. It was to have the W.D. type of rear bogie and the prototype so fitted was completed in April 1929 under the model designation R6T. This is the vehicle illustrated. It had a Dorman six-cylinder 78-h.p. side-valve petrol engine and a top gear speed of $15\frac{1}{2}$ m.p.h. Drive to the front rear wheels was taken by a sliding gear and layshaft from the main shaft. For road running, front wheel drive was disconnected. A $9\frac{1}{2}$-ton winch was fitted on the left-hand chassis side adjacent to the engine. This had 350 ft of steel wire rope and an automatic laying-on device was in-corporated. The wheel base was only 10 ft. The suspension was remarkably flexible and the rear wheels could be raised 18 in. and the front wheels 12 in. without displacing the chassis.

Resulting from the War Office trials several R6Ts were ordered in 1929. These were for use as artillery tractors towing 60-pdr. guns or 3-in. A.A. guns. They had steel bodies instead of the wood bodies of the prototype, the two spare wheels were shifted from behind the cab to the sides, and the winch was re-sited behind the cab. In addition to the gun tractors, a subsequent order was placed for recovery vehicles, the first being delivered in April 1932. These had a jib crane at the rear and stowage for salvage equipment. The drawing shows one of the recovery tractors (officially called a 'Salvage Lorry') in the early thirties towing a transporter trailer with a Light Tank Mark II. Several F.W.D. were still in service during the Second World War. The recovery vehicles were used by the B.E.F. in France until they were lost at Dunkirk, and others were used in Egypt. In commercial hands many F.W.D.s survived until quite recent years and some F.W.D.s with Roadless half-track units were used for many years as lifeboat tractors. Production vehicles had a A.E.C. 95-h.p. bus engine and in 1932 the F.W.D. firm was merged with A.E.C.

119a   **Latil TL Tractor,** 1935, France
119b   **Train Rouleur Bogie for Towed Gun Carriages,** 1935, France

For mechanising the field artillery with their 105-mm. guns, the French Artillery Test Commission at Vincennnes examined the possibility of using either the Citroen-Kegresse P.14 (Plate 112) or the Latil TL. This latter vehicle was developed specially for military use and

had four-wheel drive and crampons (shown in the drawing) which could be added to the wheel hubs when the vehicle was driven cross-country over broken ground. Tests took place in 1929 with a Somua tractor, the Citroen, and the Latil, the latter proving to be fastest and most suitable for towing the 105-mm. gun. Latil developed a 'train-rouleur' specially to fit the carriage of the 105-mm. gun. This was essentially a four-wheel bogie which fitted under the axle of the gun carriage to lift the carriage wheels free of the ground. As the wheels were of the spoked wooden type, a 'train-rouleur' was necessary to prevent them bogging down into soft mud on cross-country routes. The 'train-rouleur' was already in use for the 75-mm. gun and the similar equipment used with the 105-mm. weapon was identical except for extra leaf springs to compensate for the added weight. The Latil TL had six forward speeds and two reverse, was 4·25 metres long, 2·09 metres wide, and 1·95 metres high. It weighed 3,592 kg. It was decided to give extended troop trials to the Latil TL and one artillery regiment was equipped with a mixed group of Latils and Citroens for comparative purposes.

120   **Latil KTL Tractor,** 1936, France

While these trials were taking place, Latil brought out a modified version of their tractor under the designation KTL. This appeared in 1932, the new vehicle having larger wheels and an improved cab, though mechanically it was the same as the Latil TL. Latil proposed that that 105-mm. gun should be fitted with pneumatic tyres in place of the old spoked wheels, thus also dispensing with the need for the use of a 'train-rouleur'. Trials with the Latil KTL and a modified gun clinched the matter and in 1935 this vehicle was chosen as the new standard gun tractor for the 105-mm. gun.

121 A.D.M.K. Mulus, 1935, Austria

Produced in 1933, the A.D.M.K. (or Austro-Daimler Motor Karte) Mulus (Mule) was one of the few wheel-and-track vehicles designed which was actually successful. Most were clumsy and impractical. The Mulus was built as a carrier for the '08 pattern Maxim machine-gun. This was stowed across the body ahead of the driving position. A shield for the gun was carried at the front where the two crewmen rode. The rest of the space was given over to ammunition stowage. The Mulus had a 18-h.p. four-cylinder engine and a top speed (on wheels) of 45 km. per hour. Its combat weight was 5,060 lb. A total of 300 of these vehicles were made and from 1935–40 they equipped the machine-gun companies of Austrian infantry battalions. Later variants were built as personnel carriers with enclosed bodies. When running on tracks, the rear wheels were completely removed and stowed on brackets adjacent to the rear-mounted engine. The front axles and wheels swung forward and up to clear the ground. The length of this vehicle was 12 ft with wheels down, and the change from wheels to tracks and vice versa was effected by lifting or lowering the bogies.

122 Henschel Medium Truck, 1930, Germany

In the early thirties the German War Department evolved a subsidy scheme somewhat similar to the British one for Medium rigid six-wheelers. To broad specifications several manufacturers including Krupp, Henschel, Bussing-NAG, and Mercedes turned out six-wheel chassis with both rear bogie axles driven. The vehicles produced were used by all armed services and government departments, and were also sold commercially under the subsidy scheme. The Henschel 33G1, shown with standard War Department body, was one of the more long lived models, and, with detail changes was built for nearly 10 years from 1934. From 1938 German military vehicle production was reorganised with many models being discontinued at that time. The Henschel remained, however, and the type was also built by Magirus. The 33G1 had a 100-h.p. six-cylinder diesel engine and was also built with a petrol engine as the 33D1. It had a five-speed gearbox and was fitted with air-brakes. Overall length was 24 ft 8 in. The Henschel 33G1 was widely used until 1945, and special purpose models had bodies built for signals, workshops, engineering, bowser, and other roles. The Army designation for this vehicle was 'mittler gelandegärgig Lastkraftwagen (O)' (cross-country medium truck). The (O) indicated a basically commercial type.

123 Steyr 40D Light Truck, 1934, Austria

A special military design, this 6 × 4 vehicle was the standard Austrian Army light truck from 1935 onwards and, after Germany occupied Austria, it was also used by the German Army. The Steyr 40D had a 45-b.h.p. six-cylinder petrol engine and a top speed of 70 km.p.h. The spare wheels, carried each side of the cab were attached to the chassis frame and were free to revolve, thus giving added traction when the vehicle was crossing rough ground. The chassis was of novel type, shaped like an elongated 'Y' with the twin arms supporting the cab and engine and the long single arm supporting the body. The rear bogie was also suspended from this arm. Small steel rollers were fitted at the rear and front ends of the chassis arms to help prevent 'bellying' over rough surfaces. Twin shafts drove each pair of rear wheels. There was a seven-speed gearbox and an oil tank was sited forward of the engine with pumps to ensure adequate lubrication whatever the angle of the engine. More than 700 of these vehicles had been produced by 1937 when an uprated version, externally similar, replaced the 40D in production.

124   Horch Radio Car, Kfz 17, 1934, Germany

This small wireless car was a standard German Army type of the thirties. It consisted of a standard Horch 830 car chassis with wooden van body housing signalling equipment and extra batteries. It had a V-8 75-b.h.p. engine and was in production from 1933–35. It was also used as a staff car in open tourer form with a squared-off locker at the rear.

125   Mercedes Light Repair Car, Kfz 2/40, 1936, Germany

Another commercial car with modified body for military use this vehicle was based on the Mercedes-Benz 170V

chassis and was a widely used type. It had removable doors and a large tool locker at the back. The same vehicle could also be fitted as a wireless car with a radio in the back instead of tools. German designation was 'K1 Inst-Kw Kfz 2/40'. It had a four-cylinder 38-b.h.p. engine and was in production from 1936.

126   **Leichter Zugkraftwagen 3-ton Hl Kl 2,** 1932, Germany
127   **Sd Kfz 11 Half-Track,** 1936, Germany
128   **Sd Kfz 11/1 Nebelkraftwagen,** 1939, Germany

In the First World War, the Germans had produced a couple of lorry types which featured track units at the rear instead of wheels. After the Armistice, of course, German military activity was very much reduced as far as vehicle and equipment development was concerned. In the twenties, when much activity was devoted in France and Britain to developing half-track vehicles for military use, a few types of half-track tractors were produced in Germany for hauling guns but these were mostly wheeled vehicles fitted with conversion kits. However, they demonstrated the value of this type of vehicle and when plans for rearmament were being made in the early thirties a scheme was drawn up to develop a range of half-track trucks of varying sizes to fulfil the many military requirements for this kind of vehicle. In 1932 contracts were placed with six different automotive firms, each to produce a half-track prototype in the 1-ton, 3-ton, 5-ton, 8-ton, 12-ton, and 18-ton classes respectively. Six-cylinder or V12 engines were specified according to size, the tracks were to be as long as possible relative to the chassis, and rubber track pads were to be standard so that the vehicles could run on public roads. Overall design was in the hands of Waffen Prüfamt 6, the combat vehicle design section of the German Ordnance Department. A talented engineer named Kniepkampf did most of the work on design and in particular evolved the distinctive overlapping arrangement of the bogie wheels. The first two prototypes completed were those in the 8-ton and 3-ton class, the latter being shown here as it was built in 1932 (Plate 126). This 3-tonner was constructed by Hansa-Lloyd-Goliath, the well-known Bremen firm and was known to them as the model Hl Kl 2. Fore-runner of what became a vast family of half-tracks in the World War 2 period, it had a 3·5 l, four-cylinder engine and a standard lorry-type bonnet and front wheels. The Hl Kl 2 was mainly used for trials and later developments over the next few years led to the standard Sd Kfz 11 half-track.

The typical appearance of the Sd Kfz 11 series is shown in Plate 127. The variant illustrated is the Sd Kfz 11/1 which was a special adaptation produced from 1939 onwards to carry smoke generators, and in this form it was known as a 'Nebelkraftwagen'. Changes in the production model will be noted and include a more streamlined bonnet and mudguards and an extra axle.

129 Kfz 12 Utility Car, 1934, Germany

The German Army (Reichswehr) of the early thirties made wide use of vehicles which were basically civilian in origin. Various well-known makes of car were taken into service, and their chassis were fitted with a simple military pattern body for general service. This consisted, in fact, of a flat floor with front and rear seats, grab handles, and canvas side screens in place of doors. For inclement weather there was a conventional tourer-type canvas folding top. At the back was either a locker or a carrier frame according to role. Later vehicles in service had removable side doors, an example being shown in Plates 125 and 152. Vehicles were designated according to role, not make, and the Kfz (Kraftfahrzeug) 12 was intended as a towing vehicle for a light anti-tank gun. It carried ammunition boxes at the rear and had a towing hook. The vehicle shown is a Wanderer W11 but the Adler, Horch, and Mercedes-Benz, among others, were used in the same role and with similar bodies. A very similar type was the Kfz 11 which was a personnel (or staff) car, with a locker instead of a carrier on the back, and the Kfz 15 was a communications vehicle, similar again and with a large rear locker as shown in Plate 125 on the Kfz 2 light repair car. The Kfz 17 was a radio car with van type body, again on the same sort of medium car chassis, an example being shown in Plate 124, this time with the Horch chassis. All these vehicles had an engine up to 3 litres in capacity, the Wanderer having a six-cylinder in-line unit. Plate 152 shows the later Wanderer chassis of 1937–38 in the Kfz 11 role and affords a contrast with this earlier vehicle. By 1937–38 removable steel doors had replaced the canvas side screens.

130 and 131 Mittlerer Zugkraftwagen, Sd Kfz 6, 1936, Germany

Büssing-NAG received the contract for

the half-track in the 5-ton class and produced the prototype vehicle—designated BN 1 4 by them—in 1934. This had a Maybach NL 35 six-cylinder engine and followed the same layout as all vehicles in the half-track range. Briefly these half-tracks had a front axle and wheels with the usual Ackermann-type steering and transverse leaf springs. The main weight was carried on the tracks which stretched the full length of the vehicle aft of the bonnet. The tracks were of the highest quality, with each shoe cast and then drilled out to reduce weight. Centre-line guides were cast in to engage the bogie wheels and a rubber pad was fitted on each shoe for road running. All shoes were linked by lubricated needle bearings. A drive sprocket was carried at the front of the bogie assembly and the gearbox was situated between the engine and a short shaft to the differential and final drive. There was a dry twin-plate clutch and on all models except the 1-tonner there was a total choice of eight forward gears and two reverse, since there were alternative selections for each of the normal four gears and reverse. The steering wheel operated the front wheels in the normal way for small changes in direction but a second drop-arm was fitted in the steering box which acted after the wheel had turned a certain distance to operate the track brakes fitted at either side of the differential. So for sharp turns the appropriate track was braked to assist steering. Hand and foot brakes were fitted in the normal way and operated the track brakes and sprocket brakes respectively. The road (or bogie) wheels were pressed steel discs, four pairs each side on early models, later increased to six, all carried on torsion

bars. Idler wheels at the rear completed the suspension and these could be adjusted to tension the track.

The 5-ton half-track was intended to be an artillery tractor or assault engineer vehicle. In the latter role, as shown (top), it had four rows of seats arranged charabanc-fashion, while as a 105-mm. howitzer tractor (bottom) the rear row of seats was replaced by ammunition lockers opening up the sides. The vehicle illustrated is the BN 1 5, first production model in the 5-ton series which appeared in 1935. Later production models differed in detail and had up-rated engines but were otherwise similar. Kraus-Maffei and Daimler-Benz also built these vehicles and after Czechoslovakia was occupied in 1939 the firm of Praga also built this important type. It was a major vehicle in German service until 1945. German Army designation of 5-ton class half-tracks was Sd Kfz 6.

132 Mittlerer Zugkraftwagen Sd Kfz 7, 1937, Germany
133 Mittlerer Zugkraftwagen Sd Kfz 7/6, 1937, Germany

The half-tracks in the 8-ton class were developed by Kraus-Maffei. Early production vehicles from 1933 on were similar in appearance to the Hl Kl 2 prototype (Plate 126) but larger. The drawing shows the main production variant which appeared in 1937. This class of vehicle was used for hauling 15 cm. or 10 cm. field guns, or the 8·8 cm. Flak 18 or 36. Distinguishing features, apart from the larger size, are the spoked front wheels and the built-in ammunition locker at the back. More than 3,000 of these vehicles were built. This vehicle had a speed of 31 m.p.h.

and was 20 ft 3 in. long. The engine was a Maybach 140-h.p. six-cylinder unit. The Sd Kfz 7 was the most familiar of all the German half-tracks and was widely used during the Second World War. There were many variants, some of them armed. A typical variant is shown (Plate 130), the Sd Kfz 7/6, which was an A.A. survey vehicle and carried the crew responsible for selecting and preparing sites for anti-aircraft gun emplacements. It was known in German as a 'Flakmes-struppwagen'. The special feature was the extra large rear locker used to stow surveying equipment and tools. The Sd Kfz 7/6 first appeared in 1937.

speed was 38 m.p.h. For service use forward control was specified with a standardised GS (general service) body. The cab was open. However, A.E.C. also produced the Marshal commer-cially with enclosed normal or forward control. From 1933 all British Army orders for Medium class lorries were for the new 3-ton type. Marshals were in service by 1936 and remained in service until 1945 or even later in a few cases. Official British designation for this class of vehicle was 'Truck, 3-ton GS'. Guy, Leyland, Crossley, Karrier and Albion all built similar vehicles to this specifica-tion.

134 3-ton General Service Truck, A.E.C. Marshal, 1936–40, U.K.

In the early thirties the British Army altered their requirements in the 'Medium Rigid Six-Wheeler' class to increase the load rating from 2 to 3 tons. This was formalised in a new War Office subsidy scheme announced in 1933. Prior to this the War Office had consulted major manufacturers when the new specification was being worked out, and Leyland, Karrier Crossley and A.E.C. all built prototypes in 1932 to match the new requirements. Apart from the increase in payload, power and bodies, the general layout, complete with W.D. patent articulated rear bogie remained as before (see 107). Illustrated is the A.E.C. design, the A.E.C. Marshal, which had a four-cylinder 70-h.p. en-gine, four-speed gearbox with two-speed auxiliary, and was fitted with a 6-ton winch behind the cab with auto-matic laying-on gear. Overall length was 32 ft, the width was $7\frac{1}{2}$ ft and the Wheelbase was 12 ft $8\frac{1}{2}$ in. Top gear

135 3-ton Bridging Truck, A.E.C. Marshal, 1936–40, U.K.

This was a special purpose type on the A.E.C. Marshal chassis specifically pro-duced for Royal Engineers' bridging trains. It carried pontoons or standard F.B.E. (folding boat equipment) and the gantry-like structure was designed so that the items could be hoisted easily on and off. This type of body was also carried on other chassis in this class. Official designation was 'Truck, 3-ton, Bridging'. Introduced pre-war it was in service until 1945 and beyond.

136 Schwerer Zugkraftwagen, 12-ton, Sd Kfz 8, 1936–45, Germany

Daimler-Benz built the Sd Kfz 8 in the standard German half-track range and this large 21 ft long vehicle had a 150-h.p. Maybach V12 engine. It was intended to tow the heavy 15-cm. gun for which it used a limber to support the trail as shown. It was also used to tow the 10·5-cm. heavy A.A. gun. Ammunition was carried in the rear locker and a second vehicle carried extra rounds. The first model, the DBs 7, is shown, and was in production from 1934–36. It was superseded by later models which were similar in appearance but had uprated engines. During the war years Krupp and Skoda also built these 12-ton half-tracks and they were used post-war in the Czech Army. Sd Kfz 8 was the German Ordnance designation. The chassis layout shown for the Sd Kfz 8 is typical of all the other half-track models.

137 **Somua MCL5 Tractor,** 1936, France

Though the British had tried half-track vehicles in the early twenties (Plates 91–95), they had swiftly abandoned this type of traction for the 'rigid six-wheeler' (Plate 105) for cross-country local carrying. Not so the French, who used Kegresse half-track vehicles of various kinds right up to the Second World War. Various models of Citroen were widely used, but in 1932–33 a very efficient Somua-Kegresse, the MCG4, came into service. This was the vehicle tested with the Latil TL (Plate 119). In late 1933 an improved model, the MCL5, was produced and purchased in quantity for use both as a gun tractor and a tractor for tank transporter trailers. In this form it is seen towing the famous Somua tank. The 25-ton trailer with solid tyres was also built by Somua, specially for the tank.

138 **Somua MCL5 Artillery Tractor,** 1936, France

This illustration shows the same vehicle in the artillery tractor role for which it

was more widely used. A wood body was fitted in this case. The Somua MCL5 had a 80-h.p. four-cylinder engine with a five-speed gearbox. It weighed 5,000 kg. and could tow a 14-ton load over 1 in 5 gradients. It had a top (unladen) speed of 38·5 km. per hour. Overall length was just under 17 ft. A 2,500 kg. winch was fitted behind the cab and there was a small collapsible jib which could be erected over the tailboard for handling ammunition and stores. This can also be seen (folded flat) in Plate 137. The gun is the 155-mm. for which the Somua was the standard towing vehicle.

139 **Laffly G35T Artillery Tractor,** 1934, France

In 1935 the firm of Laffly produced a very advanced six-wheel drive tractor with articulated rear bogie. A special feature was the provision of auxiliary non-driven wheels intended to aid traction and stability on rough ground. The Laffly G35T was tested by the French Army at Vincennes and proved a powerful enough tractor to handle 155-mm. guns over the roughest going. In 1936, therefore, Laffly G35T's were ordered and this type was still in service when France capitulated in 1940. Some captured vehicles were used by the Germans.

140 **Lorraine 28,** 1936, France

In 1927 when a start was made on the mechanisation of the French cavalry divisions, they were re-organised as 'dragons porte'—literally 'carried dragoons'. Battalions were organised into machine-gun squadrons and armoured car squadrons. They were fully equipped with cross-country vehicles, initially the ubiquitous Citroen-Kegresse. In the early thirties the firm of Lorraine obtained the rights to licence-build some designs of the Czechoslovak Tatra firm. Lorraine fitted their own engine and made other detail changes. In 1933 two Tatra vehicles specially adapted for the 'dragons porte' rôle were produced for Army trials. One was a six-wheel reconnaissance car and the other, the Lorraine 28, was a 4-ton troop carrier. It had a 55-h.p. Lorraine four-cylinder engine and was about 15 ft long. Total weight was 6,500 kg.

The vehicle's top speed was 60 km. per hour and it had eight forward speeds and two reverse, these being effected by means of a four-speed gearbox with two-speed auxiliary box. The rear bogie was of the articulating, independent suspension type. The Lorraine 28 was tested in 1935 and after a few small modifications was adopted for service. With a 400 km. range, it was used by the French cavalry until France fell in 1940.

141 **Tracteur Latil TAR 5,** 1932–36, France, and
142 **Tracteur Latil TAR H,** 1932–36, France

Latil tractors had been among the earliest vehicles in service in quantity with the French artillery (Plates 65 and 66). By 1927 the Latil TAR 4 was in service, very similar to the original Latil tractor except for a new squared-off bonnet. The Latil TAR 5 was a much improved model with new steel-framed body, enclosed cab, and lower weight. It had wider wheels with chain tracks fitted round the rims. In 1932 there was a big step forward when the Latil TAR H

appeared. This had pneumatic tyres and at 4,400 kg. was 400 kg. lighter than the TAR 5 and had a much superior performance. Late in 1933 further detailed modifications were made and the designation became Latil TAR H2. This vehicle came into service in 1935 and was the standard French heavy artillery tractor until France fell in 1940.

143 **Amphibious Car, Texier de la Caillerie,** 1934, France

In June 1933 the French mechanised cavalry put out a requirement for an amphibious car. The only prototype offered by the French car industry came from a M. Texier de la Caillerie who had his design built by the firm of La Licarne. The vehicle was extremely novel in shape and had a punt-shaped chassis of duralumin with two large wheels each side. These provided the drive both on land and water and had scallop-shaped metal scoops attached to the wheel hubs to act as paddles in the water as the wheels revolved. Small wheels, one at the rear and two at the front, gave support while the vehicle was on land though these were free-running. Steering was effected by braking one of the big wheels as required, which was simple in water but made road control extremely difficult. The engine was a 6 h.p. four-cylinder unit and on land there were three forward speeds and reverse. Normal top speed was 34 km.p.h. though 60 km.p.h. could be reached, but only with excessive fuel consumption. The vehicle carried a driver and passenger only. Trials were carried out in August 1935 in the Marne and a speed of 7 km.p.h. was obtained with the current and 5 km.p.h. in still water. While the design was not impractical it proved of limited military value in the eyes of the cavalry and they abandoned interest in it in favour of a design for an amphibious light tank. This latter also proved impractical but that is beyond the scope of this present volume.

144   Scammell 6 × 4 Artillery Tractor, 1932–40, U.K.

The Scammell Pioneer was one of the longest lived of British artillery tractors. The prototype appeared in 1927 when it ran without cab top or body. It was demonstrated to members of the Imperial Conference in 1930 as one of the latest items of military equipment. Production vehicles had a cab and steel body as shown. Drive was to the rear bogie only with enclosed chain drive to the axles from the rear differential. The body sides formed seats for the gun crew and there was a steel channel gantry along the centre line of the body with a purchase for handling ammunition. To the British Army it was known as a 'Tractor 6 × 4, Heavy Artillery'. Later a heavy breakdown version was built and the chassis was also used with a tank transporter prime mover. From 1936 on, the Scammell replaced the Hathi (Plate 115) as the main heavy artillery tractor for 6-inch and 60-pdr. guns. It was also used initially to haul heavy A.A. guns.

145   Morris-Commercial   6 × 4 Artillery Tractor, 1936, U.K., and
146   Morris-Commercial 6 × 4 30-cwt Light Breakdown, 1938, U.K.

Appearing in 1936, the Morris-Com-

mercial CD/SW model was derived directly from the CD chassis (Plate 109) but the appearance was vastly different due to the adoption of the cut-away light bonnet to meet War Department requirements. Tilt and canopy folded to keep the overall height to a minimum and the special body was designed to accommodate a gun crew and ammunition. In service in 1937, the Morris artillery tractor hauled the 18-pdr. field gun and its limber. It was widely used not only by the British, but also by Australian and New Zealand artillery regiments. In 1940 the 'Quad' artillery tractor replaced the 6 × 4 vehicle for hauling field artillery and thereafter the latter type was used for towing A.A. guns. In 1939 a light breakdown model appeared on the same chassis, with a similar but different body (Plate 146). A fixed jib was attached to the rear chassis members and this was used in conjunction with the 4-ton winch which this chassis featured sited behind the cab. There were no cab doors and the overall height with tilt and canopy folded was only 6 ft 7 in. Overall length of the basic vehicle was 17 ft 2½ in. There was a six-cylinder petrol engine of 60 b.h.p. and the vehicle had five forward gears and reverse.

147   Bedford 15-cwt Truck, 1939, U.K., and
148   Bedford 15-cwt Water Tanker, 1939, U.K.

A new class of 15-cwt capacity was taken into British service in the thirties and during the World War Two period this became one of the most numerous classes in service. Most manufacturers in Britain produced vehicles in this class, usually by adaptation from their existing commercial designs. For military service a GS (General Service) body, folding canopy, and light-weight bonnet were specified. The Bedford vehicle in this 15-cwt GS class appeared in 1937 and gave a good showing at the annual military vehicle trials held by the War Office in North Wales that year. The drawing shows a production vehicle in early 1939 in the markings of the 8th Anti-Tank Battery, Royal Artillery. The 2-pdr. gun was carried *portée* fashion and special chocks and ramps were provided with the vehicle for this. The 15-cwt truck was more widely used as a platoon vehicle for infantry battalions. Folding aero-type windscreens and canvas side screens were fitted. Overall height with canopy removed was only 5 ft 3 in. The six-cylinder engine gave 64–72 b.h.p. and there were four forward gears. There was conventional drive to the rear axle. Plate 148 shows the water tanker variant on the same chassis. Instead of the GS body this featured a 200-gallon tank with two hand-operated pumps at the leading end. Vehicle shown is in the wartime markings of a Canadian armoured regiment.

149 **B.M.W. R75 Motor Cycle,** 1937–40, Germany and
150 **Zundapp KS750 Motor Cycle,** 1937–40, Germany

The German Army made wide use of motor cycle battalions in the reconnaissance role, particularly with Panzer (tank) divisions. The heavy combinations required were mostly made up of 750-cc. machines with shaft drive to the sidecar wheel, so that all wheels in the

combination were driven. The standard sidecar used had panniers for stores, carried a spare wheel, and could take a machine-gun on a pintle mount. Both the combinations shown were in service in 1939. Each had a two-cylinder horizontally-opposed engine giving 26 b.h.p.

151 **Kfz 69, Horch,** 1938, Germany

In 1937 the Germans introduced a new standard four-wheel drive chassis to replace the numerous types of utility vehicle previously in service with adapted commercial chassis. A Kubel (staff) body was mostly used but there were also ambulance and radio bodies. Horch and Auto Union were the main builders and a Horch or Ford V-8 engine was standard. A spare wheel was carried on each side, free to revolve so as to provide extra support if the vehicle 'bottomed' travelling cross-country. The Kfz 69 was used by many types of units, as a staff car, personnel carrier, or as a light artillery tractor. The doors were detachable. Early models had steering rear wheels but this was soon discontinued.

152 **Kfz 11 Utility Car,** 1938, Germany

One of many tourer type cars used by the German Army in the late thirties, this vehicle was basically a commercial type, the Wanderer W23S with a military-type body. The doors were detachable and there was a large stowage box at the rear. It was used as a staff or utility vehicle with almost any kind of military unit. It had a six-cylinder 60-h.p. engine.

153 **Morris 8-cwt Wireless Truck,**
1935–38, U.K. and
154 **Morris 15-cwt Platoon Truck,**
1935–38, U.K.

Produced as a utility-vehicle range, the
8-cwt trucks appeared in 1938 and 1939.
In the case of Morris-built examples the
engine, bonnet, axles, and other parts
were the same as for the 15-cwt range. A
standard GS body was used which could
be detached from the chassis and stood on
folding legs (visible just above the rear
mudguards) to form an office. The example shown is a wireless truck but the
personnel carrier version was externally
similar. The 8-cwt series were intended
for command and administrative units
where a big load-carrying capacity was
not required. However as they duplicated most of the features of the 15-cwt
range, the 8-cwt range was discontinued
early in World War 2. The wireless
truck had a table, two seats, and a
No. 11 radio set. The similarity to the
15-cwt truck is apparent; Plate 154
shows the latter version which was to the
same War Department specification as
the Bedford 15-cwt in Plate 147.

155 **Guy 'Ant' 15-cwt Truck,** 1935,
U.K.

The Guy-built 15-cwt truck was produced to the same specifications as the
Bedford (Plate 147) and again had the
GS body and light weight cut-away
bonnet. The chassis and engine were all
taken from Guy commercial vehicles,
only the body and wheels, etc, being
entirely new. The Guy 'Ant' actually
preceded the Bedford into service, appearing in 1935 and being issued in 1936.
It was, however, not produced in any-

thing like such great numbers as the
Bedford. The 'Ant' had a four-cylinder
Meadows engine of 55 b.h.p. and was
14 ft long. The example shown is fitted
as a line layer for the Royal Signals, with
suitably modified GS body.

156 **Guy 'Quad-Ant' Field Artillery
Tractor,** 1938, U.K.

Vehicles in the 1 ton (commercial) or
15 cwt (military) class were developed
for the British Army in the early 1930s
to meet War Office requirements, initially for light trucks for first-line infantry
use. Morris, with their model CS8
(Plate 154) and Guy, with their Ant
(Plate 155), plus Commer, with their
Beetle, were the first three firms to have
vehicles of this type in production.
Production vehicles of all three types
first appeared in the 1935 War Department motor vehicle trials and gave a
favourable performance compared with
the light six-wheelers of earlier years.
All these 15 cwt vehicles were basically
developed from commercial designs
produced by their respective manufacturers. To replace the existing six-
wheel field artillery tractors for the 18-
pdr. field gun (typified by the Morris-
Commercial CD in Plate 145), a four-
wheel drive version of the 15-cwt class
truck was requested by the War Office.
Guy produced a four-wheel drive
version of the Ant in 1937, and known as
the 'Quad-Ant', this went into production in 1938. An enclosed steel body
was provided with seating for the crew
and stowage lockers for ammunition
and battery stores. The engine was uprated to 58 b.h.p. to compensate for the
extra weight of the chassis and body.
Further ammunition was carried in the

limber which the vehicle towed to-gether with the 18-pdr. field gun. The Guy 'Quad-Ant' was the first of a new generation of four-wheel drive vehicles in the British Army and was in service in 1939; this type of vehicle was used throughout the Second World War and similar tractors of this type were later turned out by other manufacturers.

157 Mercedes-Benz G4 Staff Car, 1936, Germany

This impressive six-wheeler was pro-duced in 1933 specifically as a staff car for senior officers in the German Army and the type became familiar to the public at large since Hitler also used one as a personal transport. It had an eight-cylinder 100 h.p. engine. Also produced was a version with a 'shooting brake' body for use as a radio car. Mechanically the vehicle was based on the Mercedes 5-litre car of the period.

158 Norton Motor Cycle Combin-ation, 1938–39, U.K.

Like the Germans, the British placed great reliance on the tactical value of the motor cycle combination in the years preceding the outbreak of the Second World War. Reconnaissance regiments in armoured and mechanised cavalry brigades were partly equipped with motor cycle combinations each of which carried a Bren light machine-gun and ammunition. The idea was that these outfits would act rather like the old horsed squadrons of cavalry scouts. The Norton 633 cc. motor cycle was the standard British machine for this role, and it had a shaft drive to the sidecar wheel for good cross-country traction.

Brackets to hold the Bren gun were fitted on the right of the sidecar. Divisions of the BEF (British Ex-peditionary Force) which went to France in September–October 1939 on the outbreak of war each had recon-naissance units equipped with motor-cycle combinations, and the illustration shows a unit of the Northumberland Fusiliers, part of 50th (Northumbrian) Division. Events in the spring of 1940 quickly demonstrated the vulnerability of unprotected motor cycle combina-tions in a forward role exposed to air and tank attack, and this sort of equip-ment was rapidly withdrawn in favour of the tracked carrier.

159 Zwicky Flight Refueller, 1938, U.K.

A vehicle which came into service with the Royal Air Force in 1937 was the new 350-gallon flight refueller which was to play an important but largely over-looked role in 1940, turning round the fighters defending the skies above Britain. Built by Zwicky on a variety of chassis, the design featured a triple boom arrangement so that three fighters could be refuelled simultaneously. Shown here is a vehicle built on the Morris CD chassis (Plate 109) but the Crossley and Albion chassis were also used. The standard RAF finish of the 1938–39 period is shown.

160 GAZ-AA and
161 GAZ-AAA trucks, from 1932, Russia

Prior to 1930 there were no indigenous Russian military trucks; the few military vehicles used were imported types. The first Five Year Plan, instituted in 1928, called for the setting up of a big automotive industry to supply both commercial (ie, non-military) and military needs. At this period firms in the big industrial Western powers like Britain, Germany, and America, were taking advantage of Soviet economic expansion to secure contracts in Russia. One of the big new Russian automotive factories was built at Gorki in 1931 with American technical aid and the assistance of Ford. Known as GAZ (Gorki Automobile Zavod) (Zavod=factory), this firm produced vehicles based closely on American Ford designs. Production started in 1932 with the GAZ-A which was virtually a Russian-built copy of the American Ford Model A sedan of 1930 vintage. The first truck was the GAZ-AA which was, similarly, a copy of the American Ford Model AA 1½-ton truck. In 1933 a six-wheel version, the GAZ-AAA appeared, identical to the AA except for the twin rear bogie. Many thousands of these GAZ models were produced and they were built until 1945. In 1938 the GAZ-MM was introduced specifically for military use. This had revised squared-off mudguards and other strengthened parts. This is actually the version shown in Plate 160; however, the AA also continued in military service. Special purpose variants of the GAZ included ambulance, breakdown, anti-aircraft, and rocket-firer trucks. The GAZ had a four-cylinder 50-b.h.p. side-valve engine which, again, was copied from the Ford Model A unit. The GAZ was popularly known as the 'Russki-Ford'.

162   **ZIS-5,** from 1933, Russia

The first Russian designed truck (with a

Fiat engine) appeared in 1924 from a new factory, AMO, built in Moscow (AMO: Automobile Moscow). The first major production vehicle for military use from this factory came in 1933 by which time the plant had been renamed ZIS (Zavod Imeni Stalin: Stalin Factory). Designated ZIS-5, this vehicle complemented the GAZ-AA, but was a 2½-tonner with a six-cylinder 5-litre engine. In effect it was a scaled-up GAZ and again copied many features of contemporary American trucks in the 2½– 3-ton range. The ZIS-5 remained in production virtually unchanged until 1941 when the ZIS factory was moved in the face of the German advance into Russia. Thereafter a slightly modified design was produced in a new ZIS factory. As with the GAZ, so the ZIS was produced also in six-wheel form as the ZIS-6. Only the new twin bogie at the back differentiated it from the four-wheel version. The ZIS-5 and ZIS-6 were used for towing field guns and searchlights as well as for normal load carrying. There were also specialised breakdown, A.A. gun, and rocket-launcher versions.

163   **Isuzu Type 94,** from 1935, Japan

While Japanese military interest in motor transport dated back to the early years of the 20th Century, the few vehicles produced prior to the First World War were copied from the French Schneider truck which had been among French, British and German types imported. Japan took part in the First World War on the Allied side and in 1918 the War Department introduced a subsidy scheme similar to that operated by the British and French. Little progress was made with the development of military

The really spectacular epoch of military vehicle markings came in the First World War when the massive expansion of military forces and the huge increase in motor vehicles and military road convoys made some means of identifying military units essential for policing purposes. A secondary influence, that of morale, also affected the style of the more exotic markings which appeared, particularly in the British Army where markings were at their most colourful and complex. For security reasons symbols replaced names as a means of identifying units on both uniforms and on the associated transport vehicles. There was no formal style and identifying markings were used by units at all levels of command. **Plate 165** shows the markings of the 1st Army and 2nd Army respectively as used on their staff cars in France where these two armies formed part of the B.E.F. The 1st Army simply adopted a single white stripe painted centrally down the back of the vehicle and showing as a form of 'I'. The 2nd Army cars displayed a representation of the red/black armband worn by the division's staff officers and this was painted on the mudguards or doors of staff cars, depending on type or the whim of the driver.

Corps and Divisions tended to use more geometric signs. Originally they sometimes displayed the divisional numbers within the designs but this was disallowed for security reasons and the numbers were painted out or obliterated by a bar or square which became added as part of the sign. The two examples shown in **Plate 166,** however, are outside this category. The 14th Corps sign has symbolic origins, depicting the International Code Flag 'N', the four-

teenth letter of the alphabet. An example of its positioning on a vehicle is shown in Plate 80 which depicts a F.W.D. truck of 14 Corps in Italy in 1917. The symbol of 56th (London) Division was taken from a red sword which forms part of the Coat of Arms of the City of London. Within divisions, individual brigades, regiments, and battalions used geometric shapes in a multitude of colours to give a complex code indicating the precise function and identity of any given unit. Triangles, squares, discs, bars, rhomboids, playing-card symbols, daggers, and rectangles were among the shapes used. These were worn as cloth patches on uniforms and were often painted on unit transport so that a truck might display its divisional symbol and the symbol of the individual unit. The combinations ran to many hundreds of shapes, different for every division, and beyond the scope of this book.

Individual units also adopted cartoon-like symbols in some cases, and an example is given in **Plate 167** which shows the tailboard of a truck of 16th Auxiliary Company, Army Service Corps in 1917. The 'Britannia Penny' and the 'Penny all the Way' slogan derives from the time when the unit was wholly equipped with London buses in 1914–15 (see Plates 41–43). When the Americans entered the war in 1917 they also started to paint symbols on their vehicles and they used divisional and corps symbols (some dating back to the American Civil War) in a similar way to the British. The drawing shows the door of an infantry battalion Ford Model T car in 1918, the sign probably indicating 'B' Company. It will be noted that a War Department numbering scheme for vehicles was adopted by all combatants due to the large-scale influx of new vehicles impressed or purchased for war service which completely overwhelmed any existing civilian registration scheme. W.D. numbers have generally been allocated ever since, though the British reverted to road licence plates also after the war.

In peacetime all the colourful wartime markings were swept away and all nations adopted sober formalised marking styles again. In Britain the unit operating a vehicle was indicated in abreviated form within a white disc or oval outline on the sides of the vehicle and sometimes at the rear and front as well. An example is shown in Plate 96 where the Renault Dragon is marked as belonging to 'P' Company (P Coy) of the R.A.S.C. the unit which was responsible for troop testing new vehicle types at this period and which was based at Aldershot. In the early 1930s a new style of unit marking was adopted which dispensed with the disc outline and incorporated the vehicle's W.D. number as well in small 2-inch lettering. Shown in **Plates 168/9** are the side and tailboards of a Morris 15-cwt truck (see Plate 154) of 1st Battalion Cameron Highlanders in 1938. Not always marked was the statutory speed limit, though it is shown on this particular vehicle, as is the road licence plate. Occasionally more colourful unit markings crept in unofficially, and **Plate 168** shows an Austin 7 car of 'B' Company, 1st Battalion Scots Guards in 1938. As well as the regimental and company marking (B) on the side doors, this regiment displayed its famous cap badge on a plate affixed to the centre of the radiator front. A variation on this theme at the same period is displayed on the Bedford truck of 8th Anti-Tank Battalion, as drawn in Plate 147. In 1939 when war was declared, the British again adopted colourful divisional signs, though in a more standardised form than in 1914–18. One of the first to apply signs was 50th (Northumbrian) Division whose famous 'TT' (Tyne and Tees) emblem is shown on the Norton combination in Plate 158 at the very end of 1939.

INDEX

Note: For simplicity, cross-references in the text are made to plate (i.e. illustration) numbers only, though reference should also be made to the corresponding descriptive text where relevant.

Type	Date	Colour Plate (number)	Description (page no.)
Mercedes-Benz G4 Staff Car	1936	157	175
Mercedes Light Repair Car, Kfz 2/40	1936	125	166
Napier Light Car	1912	35/36	129
Ravaillier Amphibious Car	1910	32	128
Renault Car	1900–01	10	113
Steyr 40D Light Truck	1934	123	165
Stoewer Staff Car	1916–18	60	144
Texier de la Caillerie, Amphibious Car	1934	143	171
Trojan Light Six-Wheeler	1929	114	162
Vauxhall D Type Staff Car	1915–18	56	142
Vickers-Wolseley Staff Car	1926	100a/100b	157
White Observation Car	1917–19	72	148
White Reconnaissance Car	1917–19	71	148

5 TRACTION ENGINES AND TRACTORS (Steam, petrol and diesel, load and gun hauling)

Type	Date	Colour Plate (number)	Description (page no.)
Aveling and Porter Steam Sapper	1871	4	106
Bray Patent Traction Engine	1858	2	104
Broom and Wade 25-h.p. Military Tractor	1909	25	122
Burford-Kegresse Artillery Tractor	1926	92	154
Burrell-Boydell Traction Engine	1857	1	103
Chatillon-Panhard Tractor	1912–13	39	130
Citroen P.17 Gun Tractor	1931	111	161
Dragon Mark I Gun Tractor	1924	98	157
Dragon Mark II Gun Tractor	1926	99	157
Ford Model T Rail Tractor	1916–18	70	148
Foster-Daimler 105-h.p. Petrol Tractor	1914–18	46	134
Fowler Artillery Siege Train Traction Engine	1880	6	109
Fowler Road Locomotive	1870	5	108
F.W.D. Gun Tractor	1932	117	163
F.W.D. Tractor	1932	118	164
Government Steam Train	1870	3	104
Guy 'Quad-Ant' Field Artillery Tractor	1938	156	174
Hathi Tractor	1927–33	115-116	162
Holt 75-h.p. Petrol Tractor	1914–18	47	135
Jeffery Tractor	1915–18	50	137
Keller Tractor	1900	9	112
Laffly G35T Artillery Tractor	1934	139	170
Latil Artillery Tractor	1916–18	65	145
Latil Artillery Tractor with Delahaye Tracks	1918	66	145
Latil KTL Tractor	1936	120	164
Latil TAR 5	1932–36	141	171

Type	Date	Colour Plate (number)	Description (page no.)
Latil TAR H	1932–36	142	171
Latil TL Tractor	1935	119a	164
Latil Tractor	1916–18	61	144
Lefebvre Tractor	1913	40	131
Leichter Zugkraftwagen 3-ton Hl Kl 2	1932	126	166
McLaren 70-h.p. Traction Engine	1899	8	111
Mittlerer Zugkraftwagen Sd Kfz 6	1936	130/131	167
Mittlerer Zugkraftwagen Sd Kfz 7 and 7/6	1937	132/133	168
Morris Commercial 6×4 Artillery Tractor	1936	145	172
Pavesi Gun Tractor	1926	103	158
Pavesi P4 (and chassis)	1913	102a/102b	158
Pavesi Tractor Mark 1	1926	104	158
Renault 12-cwt Dragon	1926	96	155
Renault Porteur Tractor	1916–18	59	143
Scammell 6×4 Artillery Tractor	1932–40	144	172
Schwerer Zugkraftwagen 12 ton, Sd Kfz 8	1936–45	136	169
Sd Kfz 11 Half-Track	1936–37	127	166
Sd Kfz 11/1 Nebelkraftwagen	1939	128	166
Somua MCL5 Artillery Tractor	1936	138	170
Somua MCL5 Tractor	1936	137	170
Thornycroft 50-h.p. Heavy Oil Engine Tractor	1909	24	121
Tracteur Scotte	1894–98	7	110
Train Renard	1904	19	117
$2\frac{1}{2}$-ton Tractor	1918–19	73	148
5-ton Tractor	1918–19	74	148

6 TRANSPORT VEHICLES (Trucks and personnel carriers)

Type	Date	Colour Plate (number)	Description (page no.)
Adler 25-cwt Light Lorry	1908	22	120
A.E.C. Marshal, 3-ton General Service Truck	1936–40	134	169
Armstrong-Whitworth Military Transport Wagon	1908	21	119
Bedford 15-cwt Truck	1939	147	172
Burford-Kegresse Truck	1926	93	154
Crossley 3-ton Medium Lorry	1926	106	159
Daimler Motor Bus	1914	41	132
Dennis 3-ton Lorry (and chassis)	1913–18	54a/54b	141
Fiat 18BL Lorry	1916–18	62	145
Foden 5-ton Steam Wagon	1912	38	130
F.W.D. Artillery Supply Truck	1917–18	81	151
F.W.D. Model B 3-ton Lorry	1916–18	80	150
GAZ–AA	1932	160	175

Type	Date	Colour Plate (number)	Description (page no.)
GAZ–AAA	1932	161	175
Guy 'Ant' 15-cwt Truck	1935	155	174
Guy-Roadless 1-ton Truck	1926	95	155
Hannoversche Maschinenbau Steam Lorry	1908	18	117
Henschel Medium Truck	1930	122	165
Isuzu Type 94	1935	163	176
Jeffery 240-mm. Mortar Carrier	1918	84	151
Karrier WO6 Medium Lorry	1926	105	159
Leyland Subsidy A Type	1915–18	57	142
Leyland 3-ton Subsidy A Van	1914–18	45	134
L.G.O.C. B Type Bus/Lorry	1914–18	42	132
L.G.O.C. B Type Motor Bus	1914–18	43	133
Liberty Class B 5-ton Truck	1919	86	152
Liberty Class C 5-ton Truck (and chassis)	1920	87/88	153
Liberty Four-Wheel Drive Truck	1916–18	85	151
Milnes Daimler Motor Wagon	1906–08	17	116
Milnes Daimler Omnibus	1908–09	26	123
Morris-Commercial CD Type	1932	109	161
Morris-Commercial D Type Light Lorry	1928	107a	161
Morris 15-cwt Platoon Truck	1935–38	154	174
Morris-Roadless 1-ton Truck	1926	94	155
NAG 4-ton Lorry	1909–12	33/34	128
Napier Light Lorry	1908–09	27	123
Packard 24-h.p. 3-ton Truck	1909–18	31	127
Sautter Harlé Pigeon Van	1900–01	12	114
Schneider PB2 Omnibus	1914–18	51	138
Steyr 40D Light Truck	1934	123	165
Thornycroft Steam Wagon (Types A and B)	1901	11	113
Thornycroft 3-ton Lorry J Type (and chassis)	1913–18	55a/55b	141
T.T.S.W. 1½-ton Truck	1926	97	156
Wolseley 3-ton Lorry	1913–18	52	138
ZIS–5	1933	162	176

7 MISCELLANEOUS TYPES (Special purpose or experimental vehicles)

Type	Date	Colour Plate (number)	Description (page no.)
A.E.C. Marshal 3-ton Bridging Truck	1936–40	135	169
A7V Überlandwagen	1917–18	75	149
Bedford 15-cwt Water Tanker	1939	148	172
Citroen-Kegresse Line-Layer	1925	91	154
Citroen-Kegresse prototype	1923	90	154
Citroen P.14 Breakdown Truck	1928–32	112	161
Dodge ½-ton Light Repair Truck	1917–19	68	146
Fiat 18BL Generator Lorry	1916–18	63	145

184